BEYOND 40

THE UNFINISHED STORY REBIRTH OF A SECOND MAN

ANITA VIJ

Made with ♥ on the Notion Press Platform
www.notionpress.com

Contents

Dedication

To the men who have the courage to face their vulnerabilities,
To the families who support them,
To the women who patiently listen and offer their love,
And to all those who believe that mental health is the foundation of
a fulfilling life.
This book is for you. May it be a guide on your journey toward
understanding, growth, and inner peace.

Acknowledgements

I want to extend my deepest gratitude to everyone who has supported and inspired me throughout the journey of creating this book. This project wouldn't have come to life without the contributions, wisdom, and encouragement of many individuals who provided their valuable perspectives and experiences.

A special thanks to the men who shared their personal stories, struggles, and triumphs—your vulnerability and openness have been the heart of this book. Your willingness to explore the often-overlooked aspects of men's mental health has been a powerful catalyst for change.

I would also like to acknowledge the mental health professionals and experts who offered their knowledge and guidance, helping to shape this book's insights and provide sound advice. Your expertise has been invaluable in ensuring the content resonates and is grounded in evidence-based practices.

To my family and friends, thank you for your unwavering support and patience. You have been my emotional anchors, and your belief in the importance of this project kept me going, even when things felt overwhelming.

Lastly, to all the readers who seek growth and healing in their own journeys—this book is for you. May it spark the conversations, insights, and actions that lead to lasting change in your lives and in society.

Thank you for being part of this shared mission of promoting mental health and well-being for men in midlife. Together, we can make a difference.

Prologue

Midlife—often described as the "silent" crisis. For many men, it's a time of reflection, struggle, and, sometimes, confusion. A stage of life where everything feels like it's shifting. The body changes, relationships evolve, careers plateau, and there's this looming question: *Who am I, really?*

As we approach our 40s, society often expects men to have it all together. The successful career, the stable family life, the health, the wealth—everything neatly packaged into what we are supposed to be. But what happens when, beneath the surface of this external success, there's an internal battle? What happens when the man who has always "held it together" begins to feel the weight of invisible stress, unspoken emotions, and a creeping sense of loneliness?

This book is about that battle. It's about understanding why, as men age, mental health becomes one of the most important—and yet, most neglected—areas of their lives. We'll explore the unspoken truths about midlife transitions: the challenges, the stress, the anger, the fears, and, yes, even the joy that comes with embracing vulnerability. It's time to talk about what's often ignored: that midlife doesn't have to be a crisis; it can be a period of growth, purpose, and healing.

In these pages, you'll find stories of real men who have faced these struggles, and you'll discover the tools they've used to redefine what it means to be a man in midlife. You'll learn about the emotional expression that so often eludes men, the ways to build meaningful connections, and how to manage stress, anger, and the pressure to "provide." You'll gain insight into why men's mental health is often sidelined, how gender roles shape our emotional responses, and how we can shift those paradigms to create healthier, more fulfilling lives.

It's time to stop pretending that everything is fine when it's not. It's time to break free from the stigma around mental health and start embracing midlife as an opportunity—not a downfall. In fact, midlife can be the most transformative, rewarding stage of life—if we let it be.

This book is for the men who are struggling in silence, for those who feel like they're at the crossroads of who they were and who they want to become. It's for the women who want to better understand their partners, fathers, and brothers. And it's for anyone who believes that mental health—especially for men—is not just important, but essential.

Let's take the first step together.

Introduction: The Illusion Of Arrival

You spent the first half of your life climbing. Chasing. Building.

You were told that by the time you reach this point, you'd have it all figured out. A stable career, a family, financial security—perhaps even the wisdom that was promised to come with age. But as you stand here, on the other side of 40, there's a quiet realization creeping in: This isn't what you expected.

The world sees you as a man in control. A provider. A leader. A pillar of strength. But internally, there are questions you dare not say out loud.

"Is this it?"

"Why do I feel so disconnected?"

"Am I still relevant?"

"Have I already lived my best years?"

You are not alone in these thoughts. Every man who has walked this road before you has felt them, some in fleeting moments, others as a deep, lingering ache. Some ignored them, burying themselves in work, distractions, or quiet self-destruction. Others confronted them, stripped themselves down to their rawest form, and emerged as different men.

This book is not about escaping these questions. It is about facing them—unflinchingly, honestly, and with the courage required to step into the second half of your life with purpose.

Because here's the truth no one tells you: Midlife is not the beginning of decline. It is the threshold of reinvention.

But first, something has to die.

Why This Book? : A Personal Connection

1. The Silent Suffering of Men

Across the world, countless men struggle with mental trauma and the challenge of coping with life's demands.

The causes vary—family discord, financial stress, career struggles, or emotional neglect—yet, these issues often remain unspoken.

2. The Unequal Burden of Responsibility

In today's world, women are gaining equal rights and opportunities, yet men continue to bear the primary responsibility of providing for their families.

Society still expects men to be strong, independent, and emotionally invulnerable, even as their personal struggles go unnoticed.

3. The Freedom to Express: A Gender Divide

Women openly discuss their emotional struggles and often receive sympathy, legal support, and societal understanding.

In contrast, men hesitate to express their pain—fearing judgment, shame, and the loss of respect in their families and communities.

4. The Burden of Masculinity

From childhood, boys are taught to be tough and resilient because they are "MEN."

The phrase "Mard ko dard nahi hota" (Men don't feel pain) is deeply ingrained in Indian culture and beyond.

But is it really true? Do men not feel emotions as deeply as women?

They do. They feel pain, heartbreak, and rejection. They cry too—just behind closed doors.

5. The Pressure to Provide & the Cost of Failure

A man is expected to provide financial security, a stable home, and a good lifestyle for his family.

If he struggles financially or emotionally, he is often criticized, ridiculed, or abandoned—sometimes even by his own wife and children.

The relentless pressure can lead to stress, anxiety, and depression, pushing many men to self-destruction or even suicide.

Why This Must Change

It is time to acknowledge that **men, too, need emotional support, validation, and an outlet to express their pain.**

This book is a step towards breaking the silence and offering men **the guidance and strength they need to navigate life beyond 40**.

Women, please don't get furious —after all, you already know you are naturally gifted in handling emotions, relationships, and life's ups and downs. This book isn't about undermining that; rather, it's about giving men the tools to navigate their own struggles, which are often overlooked or left unspoken. If anything, this book might just help the men in your life become better partners, fathers, and friends!

What This Book Offers

A Voice for Men's Mental Health

This book sheds light on the **silent struggles men face after 40**—challenges that are rarely discussed but deeply felt.

It provides a **safe space** to acknowledge emotions, address fears, and understand the mental shifts that come with aging.

Real-Life Stories & Case Studies

The book includes **true experiences of men** who have battled stress, loneliness, and midlife crises.

These stories will help readers relate and **realize they are not alone** in their journey.

Understanding the Midlife Transition

Why do men **experience emotional turmoil after 40?**

How do **biological, psychological, and societal** factors contribute to stress and anxiety?

The book explores these questions and offers **practical insights** into navigating this phase.

Solutions & Strategies for Mental Well-being

From **stress management techniques to emotional resilience,** the book provides **actionable steps** to help men regain control over their lives.

Topics include **therapy, meditation, fitness, career shifts, relationships, and finding new purpose in life.**

A Guide to Thriving, Not Just Surviving

This book is not just about understanding problems—it's about **solving them.**

By the end, readers will gain **clarity, confidence, and the courage to rebuild their lives with strength and purpose.**

Male vs. Female Coping Strategies

A lighthearted but insightful comparison of how men and women handle midlife stress.

Offering a balance—how men can learn from women's emotional expression while maintaining their sense of self.

A Guided 30-Day Plan for Mental Well-Being

A structured month-long plan with daily tasks focused on emotional, physical, and social well-being.

This could include mindfulness exercises, relationship improvement tasks, or social connection challenges.

The Role of Faith and Belief Systems

How faith (regardless of religion) can provide solace, direction, and a sense of belonging in difficult times.

Ancient wisdom on mental resilience from Hindu, Buddhist, and other philosophical traditions.

Why It's Important

Men and women experience **hormonal changes differently** (andropause vs. menopause).

Their **coping mechanisms vary** (men often internalize stress, women tend to express and seek support).

Societal expectations affect their mental health in distinct ways (men are pressured to be "strong" and "providers," while women juggle multiple roles and emotional responsibilities).

A Message To The Reader: You Are Not Alone

If you have ever felt **lost, stressed, or emotionally drained**, know that **millions of men feel the same way.**

This book is here to **acknowledge your struggles, validate your emotions, and offer solutions.**

It's Okay to Ask for Help?

Seeking support **does not make you weak—it makes you human.**

Whether it's through **therapy, friendships, or self-reflection,** healing begins when you open up.

Your Story Is Still Being Written

Life **after 40 is not an end—it's a new chapter full of possibilities.**

You have the power to **reshape your mindset, relationships, and future.**

Take the First Step
Change doesn't happen overnight, but **small steps lead to big transformations.**

This book is your **companion in the journey to rediscovering** happiness, peace, and purpose.

CHAPTER ONE

Understanding Mental Health After 40

1. Why Men's Mental Health After 40 Matters:

When it comes to mental health, society often focuses on women's experiences, leaving men's mental health needs overlooked, especially as they reach midlife. However, the reality is that men in their 40s face a unique set of challenges that can profoundly affect their well-being—physically, emotionally, and mentally. Understanding why these experiences differ from women's, and why it's essential to discuss mental health specifically for men after 40, is crucial to breaking the stigma and promoting better mental health care.

1. Societal Expectations and the Pressure to Be Strong

From an early age, men are often taught to be the "providers," "protectors," and "stoic figures" in society. They are conditioned to mask their emotions, suppress vulnerability, and avoid discussing mental health struggles. This cultural expectation can have a detrimental impact on mental well-being, especially as they reach midlife. In their 40s, men often find themselves caught between the pressures of career success, raising families, and facing the changes that come with aging. All of this, combined with the societal notion that men must always remain "strong," can result in feelings of isolation, frustration, and an inability to seek help when it's needed most.

2. Physical Changes and Mental Health

The physical changes men undergo after 40, including a decline in testosterone, can contribute to feelings of fatigue, low energy, and loss of confidence. These shifts often trigger mental health concerns such as depression, anxiety, and irritability. However, unlike women, who are generally more likely to openly discuss their emotional and physical changes, men often remain silent about their struggles, which can lead to unaddressed mental health issues. These hormonal and physical shifts, coupled with the lack of open dialogue, can leave men feeling disconnected from their bodies and, ultimately, themselves.

3. The Midlife Crisis and Emotional Re-evaluation

A common experience for men in their 40s is the "midlife crisis," where they begin to reevaluate their life choices, accomplishments, and purpose. This often leads to a crisis of identity and a sense of loss or uncertainty. Unlike women, who may have more societal support to explore their emotions and seek personal growth, men may feel pressured to remain "on track" and suppress their feelings of doubt and confusion. This can result in significant emotional strain, leading to mental health challenges such as anxiety, depression, and a sense of unfulfilled potential.

4. Family Dynamics and Relationship Stress

Midlife often brings shifts in family dynamics. Men may experience changes in their relationships with their children, spouse, or aging parents. They may struggle with the empty nest syndrome as their children grow older and leave home, or they may feel disconnected from their spouse after years of juggling responsibilities. Additionally, men are more likely to face challenges like job loss, career shifts, or financial strain at this stage, all of which can further strain their mental health. Women may have more social networks to lean on during these transitions, but men often face these challenges alone, without the emotional support they need to navigate the difficulties of midlife.

5. The Importance of Opening the Dialogue

Talking about men's mental health after 40 is essential not only for improving their well-being but also for changing societal narratives around masculinity. By normalizing the discussion of mental health, we can empower men to seek help, talk about their struggles, and embrace their vulnerabilities. Mental health is not a gendered issue—it's a human issue. The more we encourage open conversations, the more men will feel empowered to take control of their mental health, rather than suffer in silence.

6. Why It's Time for Change

For too long, men's mental health has been a taboo subject, sidelined in favor of traditional expectations. But the truth is, men's experiences in midlife are unique, and they deserve to be addressed with the same care, understanding, and attention as women's. Mental health should never be something men feel they must hide or conquer alone. By focusing on this issue, we can help break the stigma, provide the support men need, and ensure that men in their 40s can live fulfilling, balanced, and mentally healthy lives.

2. The Midlife Shift

Understanding physical, emotional and mental shifts

Here's an overview of these shifts:

Physical Shifts:

1. **Slower Metabolism:** Many men notice weight gain, especially around the abdomen, due to a slower metabolism. This can lead to frustration, as it requires more effort to maintain a healthy weight.

2. **Changes in Energy Levels:** Reduced energy and stamina are common as muscle mass naturally decreases with age. This can impact both physical activities and day-to-day productivity.

3. **Decline in Testosterone:** Testosterone levels typically begin to decline around the age of 40, which can lead to lower libido, reduced muscle mass, and an increase in body fat. This is often a significant source of concern for men as they age.

4. **Joint and Muscle Pain:** As the body ages, cartilage begins to wear down, leading to more aches and pains, especially in the joints. Regular physical activity can mitigate some of this discomfort, but it can be a reminder of the aging process.

5. **Sleep Issues:** Changes in sleep patterns are common, including insomnia or interrupted sleep. This can be linked to hormonal shifts, stress, or other physical conditions that often emerge at this age.

6. **Vision and Hearing Changes**: Presbyopia (difficulty focusing on close objects) and gradual hearing loss are normal parts of aging that many men experience during their 40s.

Emotional Shifts:

1. **Re-evaluation of Life's Purpose**: Men in their 40s often experience what some refer to as a "midlife crisis." They may start reflecting on their past achievements, what they've accomplished, and whether they're living the life they had envisioned. This can lead to feelings of dissatisfaction or confusion.

2. **Relationship Strains**: Emotional changes can affect personal relationships. Some men may feel disconnected from their partners or families due to a shift in priorities. The re-evaluation of life goals can create tension in marriages or close friendships.

3. **Fear of Aging**: The realization that life is half over (or more) can evoke anxiety about aging. This may manifest as a fear of losing physical abilities, opportunities for new experiences, or facing the reality of death.

4. **Increased Responsibility**: With aging parents and growing children, men often feel the emotional weight of being a "caretaker" both for their families and financially. This added pressure can lead to stress and emotional fatigue.

Mental Shifts:

1. **Cognitive Decline**: While it's not always the case, some men experience a slight decline in cognitive function after 40, such as memory lapses, slower thinking, or difficulty concentrating.

This can be attributed to various factors like stress, sleep deprivation, or hormonal changes.

2. **Desire for Career Change or Stability**: Men often start re-assessing their careers in their 40s. Some may feel stuck in their jobs, while others may long for a new challenge or a complete career change. This mental shift can bring about both excitement and anxiety.

3. **Feeling of loneliness and isolation:**Many men in their 40s experience feelings of loneliness or isolation, even when surrounded by family and friends. This often stems from a lack of deep emotional connections, as they may not have invested as much time in nurturing relationships with relatives or their children due to work commitments and other responsibilities. Unlike women, who often maintain strong connections with friends, relatives, and their children, men may struggle with a sense of disconnection. Women at this stage tend to keep themselves engaged in these relationships, reducing the feelings of isolation. In some cases, even husband and wife may feel a sense of distance, longing for the closeness they once shared in their younger years, before the weight of responsibilities took its toll.

4. **Increased Self-Awareness**: Men in their 40s might become more introspective. They're more likely to think deeply about their personal values, the legacy they want to leave, and their relationships with others. This shift can bring a renewed sense of purpose, but also discomfort if they feel they haven't achieved enough.

5. **Increased Anxiety and Stress**: With aging comes an increased awareness of mortality and life's unpredictability, which can lead to more anxiety and stress. This may also be compounded by the pressure to meet financial and personal expectations.

Why These Shifts Matter:

Understanding these shifts—whether physical, emotional, or mental—is crucial. Midlife can be a time of significant challenge, but it also offers an opportunity for reflection and personal growth. Navigating these changes with awareness, self-compassion, and healthy coping mechanisms can make all the difference for a man's mental and emotional well-being.

3. Navigating Change

Understanding Midlife Transitions: Career Changes, Relationship Dynamics, and Family Responsibilities

Midlife is often a time of significant transitions, where men face shifts not only in their physical health but also in their careers, relationships, and family roles. The pressure of these changes can bring about profound emotional and mental effects, but they also offer an opportunity for growth and self-discovery.

1. **Career Changes**: By the time men reach their 40s, they often begin reflecting on their professional lives. Some may feel dissatisfied or stagnant in their careers, seeking new challenges, while others may feel an overwhelming pressure to remain successful, despite changing personal values. A career shift can evoke both excitement and anxiety, and for some, it may be an opportunity to pursue passions that were set aside earlier in life.

2. **Relationship Dynamics**: In midlife, many men find that their relationships with spouses, children, and friends evolve. While relationships with children may become more complex as they transition into adolescence or adulthood, the dynamics within marriages can shift as well. The sense of youthful romance may be replaced with a focus on practicalities, creating a sense of distance. The emotional disconnect that sometimes occurs can lead to frustration or a longing for the intimacy of earlier years for one or both the spouses. Which can create problems as a life devoid of love cannot sustain itself for long.

3. **Family Responsibilities:** At this stage, many men take on added responsibilities in caring for aging parents or supporting their children through major life milestones, like funding their education in foreign country. Balancing these demands with the pressures of work and a disturbed personal life can be overwhelming. In many cases, the role of the "caretaker" becomes central, both emotionally and financially, which can lead to feelings of exhaustion and a lack of time for self-care.

Midlife can be both a time of crisis and a chance for renewal. By understanding these transitions and adjusting expectations, men can better navigate the challenges and seize opportunities for personal fulfillment.

4. Coping with Unexpected Challenges: Divorce, Job Loss, and Empty Nest Syndrome

Life in your 40s can bring unexpected challenges that shake your sense of stability and well-being. Whether it's the end of a long-term relationship, the loss of a job, or adjusting to an empty nest as children grow independent, these transitions can trigger feelings of loss, anxiety, and confusion. However, these challenges also provide an opportunity to redefine yourself and find new ways to navigate life with resilience and hope.

1. **Divorce**: The end of a marriage or long-term relationship can be one of the most emotionally and financially challenging experiences of midlife. Feelings of failure, rejection, and loneliness often accompany the separation. However, this period can also serve as a catalyst for personal growth. By focusing on self-care, rebuilding one's identity, and learning to embrace new beginnings, men can regain a sense of control and rediscover their passions and independence.

2. **Job Loss**: Losing a job in your 40s can feel like a significant blow to your identity, especially if you've dedicated years to a particular career. Along with the emotional distress, financial pressures may mount, creating additional stress. Yet, job loss can also open doors to new opportunities. This transition is a chance to reassess career goals, explore new interests, and perhaps take risks that were not previously considered. It's important to view this period not as an ending, but as a chance for reinvention.

3. **Empty Nest Syndrome**: As children leave home to pursue their own paths, many parents experience a profound sense of loss. The once-busy household suddenly feels quiet, and parents may

struggle with a sense of purpose or direction. In these moments, it's crucial to rediscover personal interests, strengthen relationships, and redefine the family dynamic. While the transition to an empty nest can be tough, it can also offer a chance to reconnect with a spouse, focus on personal growth, and embark on new adventures.

5. Strategies for Dealing with Uncertainty and Finding Stability

1. **Self-Reflection and Acceptance**: Taking time to reflect on what's working and what's not can help men develop a more balanced perspective on life. Acceptance of the current situation—rather than resisting it—can help reduce stress and open the door to positive change.

2. **Building a Support System**: Reaching out to trusted friends, family, or support groups can provide emotional grounding. Sharing feelings with others who understand your experiences can help mitigate feelings of isolation.

3. **Embracing Flexibility and Adaptability**: Life is full of uncertainties. Adopting a mindset that embraces change and flexibility can reduce feelings of anxiety. Developing coping skills like mindfulness, meditation, and stress management techniques can also help maintain emotional balance during times of uncertainty.

Turning necessity into choice is the key to success in life.

6. The Mind-Body Connection

You've heard the saying, "*A healthy body leads to a healthy mind,*" but what does that really mean for you? The connection between physical health and mental well-being is undeniable—and stronger than you might think. Physical activity doesn't just help you look and feel better; it's a powerful tool for boosting your mood, reducing stress, and enhancing your mental clarity.

When you engage in regular exercise, your brain releases feel-good chemicals like endorphins and serotonin. These natural mood boosters can help you combat anxiety, depression, and stress, leaving you with a sense of calm and control. But it's not just about the rush—consistent physical activity also improves cognitive function, sharpens focus, and helps you sleep better, which in turn promotes emotional stability.

In short, prioritizing your physical health isn't just about staying in shape—it's about creating a solid foundation for a resilient, balanced mind. Start moving, and watch how your mental well-being follows suit.

Hormonal Shifts and Mental Health: Navigating Menopause and Andropause

Hormonal changes during midlife are a natural part of the aging process, but they can have a profound impact on mental health. For both women and men, this stage can bring about emotional and psychological challenges, often linked to the shifts in hormones like estrogen, progesterone, and testosterone.

1. **Menopause in Women:** For women, menopause marks the end of their reproductive years, typically occurring in their late 40s or early 50s. As estrogen levels fluctuate and eventually decline, it can bring about a range of emotional and mental health changes. Many women report experiencing increased mood swings, irritability, anxiety, and even feelings of depression during this time. The hormonal imbalance can also affect sleep patterns, leading to insomnia and fatigue, further exacerbating stress levels. These emotional challenges can impact relationships, work, and overall quality of life.

   However, menopause is not only about loss—it's also an opportunity for growth. Understanding that these changes are temporary and finding ways to manage stress, such as through exercise, mindfulness, or therapy, can help women maintain emotional balance and thrive during this transition.

2. **Andropause in Men:** Andropause, often referred to as "male menopause," is the gradual decline in testosterone levels that typically occurs in men as they age, usually beginning around the age of 40. While not as abrupt as menopause, this gradual decrease can lead to physical, emotional, and mental changes. Men may experience symptoms such as fatigue, irritability, low libido, mood swings, and difficulty concentrating. These changes can contribute to feelings of frustration, anxiety, and even depression, as men may struggle with the sense of losing their vitality or not measuring up to societal expectations of masculinity.

   Much like women, men can benefit from understanding and accepting these natural shifts in their bodies. By prioritizing their physical health, staying active, and seeking emotional support when needed, men can mitigate the mental health effects of andropause and feel more in control of their lives.

3. **The Link Between Hormonal Changes and Mental Well-being:** Both menopause and andropause show us how closely our physical and mental health are intertwined. Hormonal imbalances can bring about significant shifts in mood, cognition, and overall emotional stability. However, recognizing that these changes are natural can help reduce the stigma around them and encourage healthier coping mechanisms.

Whether through lifestyle changes, seeking therapy, or simply allowing oneself the grace to navigate these years with patience, managing hormonal changes with an open mind can lead to a more positive and fulfilling experience of midlife.

CHAPTER TWO

Emotional Well-Being and Relationships

So far, we've tackled these topics with all the seriousness of a financial advisor discussing retirement plans. But let's be honest—life, especially after 40, is anything but a straight-faced affair. Now, let's loosen up a bit, add some humor, and dive into the wonderfully chaotic world of emotions and relationships. After all, if we can't laugh about it, we might just end up stress-eating an entire pizza instead!

1. Emotional Expression and Resilience

Why Men Bottle It Up and Women Let It Out (Loudly!)

Let's face it—when it comes to emotions, men and women seem to be playing entirely different sports. Women are in a professional tennis match, gracefully (or sometimes not-so-gracefully) volleying their emotions back and forth, openly discussing feelings, crying when needed, and hugging it out afterward. Men, on the other hand, are in a no-contact wrestling match with their emotions—trying to pin them down, lock them away, and pretend they never existed in the first place.

Why Men Struggle with Emotional Expression

Imagine this: A man and a woman are both having a tough day. The woman calls her best friend and immediately starts with, *"You won't believe what happened today!"* The conversation goes on for an hour, covering every detail—what was said, how it was said, what she should have said, and a breakdown of the offender's astrological sign to explain their terrible behavior. By the end of it, she feels relieved, validated, and ready to move on.

Now, let's look at the man. He gets home after a tough day, sits on the couch, stares at the TV, and when his wife asks, *"What's wrong?"* he says, *"Nothing."* Nothing?! He's just had a brutal day, his boss yelled at him, his lower back is aching, and he just realized he forgot to pay the electricity bill. But instead of talking about it, he decides to keep it all inside, hoping it'll just disappear like an unwanted pop-up ad.

This, my friends, is the great *Emotional Expression Gap*.

The Consequences of Bottling It Up

Suppressing emotions is like trying to hold in a sneeze—it might seem like a good idea at the moment, but sooner or later, it's going to explode in a way that isn't pretty. Men who constantly suppress their emotions may seem calm on the outside, but internally, they're carrying around years of built-up stress, frustration, and unspoken feelings. And when that dam finally bursts? Well, that's how you get a middle-aged man suddenly buying a motorcycle he has no business riding.

Not expressing emotions can lead to serious mental health issues like anxiety, depression, and even physical health problems. It's no coincidence that men over 40 are at higher risk for heart disease—turns out, stuffing your emotions down like an overfilled suitcase isn't the best long-term strategy.

How Men and Women Differ in Coping Mechanisms

Men and women handle emotions differently, and that's not necessarily a bad thing—except when one side refuses to acknowledge they even *have* emotions.

- **Women talk, men retreat:** Women process emotions by talking, analyzing, and often venting to their support system. Men, on the other hand, tend to withdraw—maybe they'll fix something around the house, hit the gym, or disappear into a YouTube rabbit hole of *"Top 10 Greatest Sports Moments"* just to avoid dealing with their feelings.

- **Women cry, men punch things (or hold it in):** A woman having a bad day might cry, let it out, and move on. A man having a bad day? He might punch a pillow, grunt loudly at the news, or just sit in complete silence, staring at the wall like a malfunctioning robot.

- **Women seek comfort, men seek distraction:** A woman upset about something might call her sister, eat some chocolate, and watch a rom-com that makes her cry even more (somehow, this helps). A man in the same situation will likely drown his emotions in work, alcohol, or an obsessive new hobby—suddenly, he's an expert in woodworking and can't explain why.

The Solution? Find a Middle Ground

The truth is, men don't have to turn into poetry-reading, tear-sharing, emotional philosophers overnight—but they *do* need to find healthier ways to express their feelings. It can be as simple as:

Talking to a trusted friend or partner (even if it's just *"Yeah, today sucked."*)
Writing down thoughts in a journal (yes, men can have journals too!)
Engaging in activities that allow emotional release—sports, meditation, or even just belting out a song in the car (no judgment).

The key is realizing that expressing emotions doesn't make a man weak—it makes him *human*. And trust me, no one wants to be that guy who explodes over a misplaced remote control just because he's been holding in years of stress.

So, to all the men out there: It's okay to talk. It's okay to feel. And no, you don't need to buy a motorcycle just to prove you're still in control of your life.

2. Relationships in Midlife

Why Your 40s Feel Like a Social Puzzle You Forgot How to Solve

By the time a man reaches his 40s, relationships—whether with his spouse, friends, or kids—start to feel like an old mobile phone plan. At first, everything was unlimited, exciting, and full of possibilities. But somewhere along the way, the fine print changed, and now you're stuck wondering why your connection keeps dropping.

Let's dive into how midlife changes the relationship game for men—and how women, as usual, seem to have figured it out way before men.

Marriage: From Fireworks to Wi-Fi Connection

Remember the early days of marriage? Long conversations, spontaneous dates, texting *"I miss you"* just 20 minutes after leaving the house? Fast forward to your 40s, and now your most common text to your wife is, *"Did you pay the electricity bill?"*

The romance isn't gone—it's just... evolved. In your 20s and 30s, love felt like a Bollywood movie. In your 40s, it's more like a reliable Wi-Fi connection—you don't always notice when it's working, but the moment it stops, everything falls apart.

And while men tend to focus on providing stability, women prioritize *connection*. That's why your wife still remembers your anniversary in excruciating detail while you're just proud you remembered which month it's in.

How to Keep the Spark Alive?

Surprise her once in a while—no, not by forgetting her birthday.

Actually listen when she talks. Nodding while watching TV doesn't count.

Remember that small gestures matter. A random *"You look nice today"* can go a long way (as long as you don't say it while she's in pajamas and a hair towel).

Friendships: From Bros to Ghosts

Men's friendships in their 20s and 30s are simple: "You like cricket? I like cricket! We're best friends now." Fast forward to the 40s, and those same friendships have been replaced by *occasional* WhatsApp forwards and a yearly *"We should catch up"* text that leads nowhere.

Meanwhile, women in their 40s are basically running their own emotional support empires. They have brunch groups, yoga partners, old college WhatsApp groups that *actually* stay active, and at least three friends who know everything about their life—including what their husband said last Tuesday that annoyed them.

Why Do Men Lose Friends in Midlife?

Work takes over, and "hanging out" starts to feel like a luxury.

Family responsibilities increase, and suddenly, a night out requires government-level planning.

Somewhere along the way, *talking about feelings* started to sound harder than just watching sports in silence.

The Fix? Make an Effort.

Text an old friend. And this time, *actually* meet up.

Find hobbies that involve socializing (poker, golf, or even just a walk).

Accept that friendship takes effort—just like everything else in your 40s.

Parenting: From Hero to ATM

Remember when your kids were little and thought you were the strongest, smartest, most amazing person on the planet? Yeah, that ends sometime around their teenage years.

Now, your main roles are:

1. **Financial sponsor** – *"Dad, I need money."*
2. **Taxi driver** – *"Dad, can you drop me off?"*
3. **Wi-Fi fixer** – *"Dad, the internet isn't working!"*

Meanwhile, your wife somehow still maintains a deep, emotional connection with the kids. She knows their friends, their favorite songs, and what they're stressed about. You? You just found out last week that your son changed schools... two years ago.

How to Stay Connected?

Actually **listen** when they talk, even if it's about things you don't understand (yes, that includes their weird music choices).

Do things *together*—sports, cooking, or even just watching a movie *they* like for once.

Show them that you care, not just with money, but with time.

3. Why Women Handle Relationships Better in Midlife

While men struggle to keep friendships alive and figure out how to bond with their kids, women seem to glide through midlife like relationship ninjas.

They call their friends *just because*. They maintain emotional closeness with their kids. They have multiple WhatsApp groups that actually *respond to messages*.

The secret? They **invest time.**

Men often treat relationships like old appliances—expecting them to work forever without maintenance. Women, on the other hand, treat relationships like houseplants—they water them, nurture them, and actually check if they need attention.

Final Thoughts: Keep the Connection Alive

Midlife isn't about losing relationships; it's about adapting to them. Your friendships, marriage, and parenting may look different than before, but that doesn't mean they can't be fulfilling.

Talk more—To your wife, your parents, your kids, and your friends.

Make time—Yes, even if it's just a 30-minute coffee

Catch-up.

Appreciate what you have—Because let's be honest, you wouldn't survive without them.

And remember: *Life in your 40s isn't about trying to be 25 again. It's about making sure you don't become that old guy who only talks to his dog.*

CHAPTER THREE

Career and Identity crises

1. The Impact of Career and Identity

Why Your Job Title Feels Like Your Last Name After 40

Picture this: You're at a party, meeting someone new. The conversation starts like this—

Person: *"Hey, nice to meet you! So, what do you do?"*

You: *"I'm a [computer engineer]."*

And just like that, your entire existence has been summed up in a few words.

Men in their 40s often feel like their identity is directly tied to their careers. Promotions feel like gold medals, job losses feel like personal failures, and retirement? That sounds like an existential crisis waiting to happen.

Meanwhile, women—though equally ambitious—seem to have a broader perspective. They find identity not just in work, but in friendships, family, hobbies, and *somehow* remembering every birthday of every cousin they've ever had.

So, what happens when men hit their 40s and suddenly start questioning their place in the world? Let's explore.

Career Success: The Sweet Trap of "I've Made It"

For men, career success in their 40s often feels like reaching the top of a mountain—only to realize there's a whole new range to climb.

Take Raj, for example. Raj spent his 20s and 30s grinding hard, climbing the corporate ladder, missing family dinners, and sacrificing weekends. He finally lands the *VP of Something Important* title, complete with a fancy office and a chair that doesn't squeak.

But here's the plot twist: Raj thought reaching the top would bring him endless satisfaction. Instead, he finds himself thinking—*Is this it?*

That's the problem with tying your entire identity to a job. The moment the excitement of achievement wears off, you're left wondering, *Now what?*

How to Avoid the "Success Hangover"

Realize that your job is what you *do*, not who you *are*.

Invest in hobbies that aren't tied to work (no, checking LinkedIn doesn't count).

Spend more time with people who love you for *you*, not your title.

Because at the end of the day, no one's tombstone ever said, *"He was really great at Excel spreadsheets."*

2. Career Struggles: When Things Don't Go As Planned

Now, let's talk about the flip side—what happens when your career *doesn't* go as expected?

Meet Vinay. At 42, he was let go from a job he had for over a decade. One day, he had a stable income, a well-rehearsed work routine, and a clear sense of purpose. The next day, he was refreshing his email inbox every five minutes, hoping for a job offer that never came.

Men often struggle more with career setbacks because society has conditioned them to believe that *providing* equals *self-worth*.

Signs You're Having a Career Identity Crisis

You introduce yourself as your "former" job title.

You feel personally attacked when someone asks, *"So, what's next?"*

You start Googling *"At what age is it too late to become a pilot?"*

But here's the truth: Losing a job doesn't mean losing yourself. It's an opportunity to pivot, rediscover passions, and maybe even do something completely different.

How to Bounce Back

Don't isolate yourself—talk to people, network, and (begrudgingly) update your résumé.

See this as a *transition,* not an *end*—careers aren't straight roads; they're roller coasters.

Remember that failure isn't a tattoo, it's a temporary sticker.

3. Men vs. Women: Who Handles Career and Identity Shifts Better?

If men are like racehorses charging full speed ahead, women are more like marathon runners—they pace themselves, find joy in the journey, and somehow manage to hold conversations while running.

Men often define themselves by their **job title and earnings**.

Women, while equally ambitious, tend to draw identity from **multiple sources**—career, relationships, personal growth, and sometimes an entire side business selling handmade jewelry on Instagram.

That's why when a man loses his job, he feels like he's lost *himself*. When a woman faces the same challenge, she may take a step back, cry over a tub of ice cream, *then* figure out her next move.

The Lesson? Diversify Your Identity Portfolio

Men in their 40s should start expanding their sense of self beyond work.

Build **stronger personal relationships** (your college best friend won't care about your job title).

Explore **interests outside of work** (because nobody wants to retire with no hobbies except refreshing email).

Accept that **change is normal**—just like your hairline, some things will shift whether you like it or not.

Final Thoughts: Your Job is Not Your Legacy

When you're 80 years old, sitting on your porch with a cup of tea (or whiskey, no judgment), you won't be reminiscing about your *quarterly reports.*

You'll remember:

The relationships you built.

The adventures you took.

The *person* you became, beyond your job title.

So, if you're in your 40s and questioning your career or identity, don't panic. You're not lost—you're just evolving. And trust me, *midlife isn't a crisis—it's just the next chapter.*

Now, go update that résumé... and maybe pick up a hobby that doesn't involve PowerPoint.

CHAPTER FOUR

Loneliness and Social Isolation

1. Why Men May Face Increased Loneliness in Midlife (And Why Women Are Better at Avoiding It)

Let's be honest—if friendship were a sport, women would be playing an intense, never-ending game of doubles tennis, complete with synchronized tea breaks, group chats that never die, and emergency "venting" sessions at a moment's notice. Men? Men are more like lone wolves who occasionally bump into an old buddy at the grocery store and grunt, "We should catch up," knowing full well neither of them will ever text first.

But here's the catch—midlife is when that lone-wolf strategy starts backfiring.

The Disappearing Act of Male Friendships

Men in their 40s often wake up one day and realize their **social circle has mysteriously shrunk**—like a wool sweater tossed in a hot dryer. What happened? Well, life happened. Career demands, family responsibilities, and the slow but steady erosion of friendships that were once built on weekly beer nights and casual meetups.

Unlike women, who actively **nurture friendships**, men tend to bond over **shared activities** rather than deep conversations. It's easy to have friends when you're playing on the same cricket team or grabbing drinks after work, but what happens when work stress, family obligations, or sheer exhaustion start getting in the way? Suddenly, that solid group of guy friends turns into **a few names buried in the contacts list**, last messaged in 2018.

Men vs. Women: The Social Network Battle

Women have **a built-in support system**—whether it's their sisters, childhood friends, book clubs, or even the random woman they just met in the restroom but now consider their "soul sister." They **talk, share, and process emotions** together.

Men? Not so much. A typical **male friendship maintenance** conversation goes something like this:

Rehan: "Hey man, it's been a while."
Amit: "Yeah, busy with work."
"Same here. We should catch up."
"Yeah, let's do that sometime."
"Cool."
"Cool."
(Neither follows up.)

Meanwhile, **women's conversations** look more like:

Sarah: "Hey, how are you?"
Lina: "Omg, let me tell you EVERYTHING that happened this

week."
(Three hours and 172 voice messages later, their bond is even stronger.)

The Mental Health Risks of Male Loneliness

Social isolation is no joke—it can lead to:

Increased stress and anxiety

Higher risk of depression

Higher rates of heart disease and even early mortality

In short, **friendship isn't just about fun—it's about survival.** Science backs this up: studies show that **men with strong social connections live longer, healthier lives** compared to those who isolate themselves.

How Men Can Build (and Maintain) Friendships in Midlife

Let's face it—no one wants to be the guy who suddenly sends "Let's hang out!" texts out of nowhere and gets ignored. So how do men rebuild or strengthen their friendships in their 40s?

Make friendships part of your routine. Plan monthly meetups, whether it's a coffee, a game of squash, or even just a group chat where you actually **reply.**

Join something. A fitness group, a weekend biking club, a community project—men bond best when they're **doing something together.**

Be the first to reach out. No, it's not weird to text an old friend and ask how they're doing. Just do it—you might be surprised how many are feeling the same loneliness but are too hesitant to make the first move.

Open up (a little). You don't need to spill your deepest emotions, but talking about **real** things beyond sports scores and work stress will strengthen connections.

Final Thoughts: Don't Be the Lone Wolf

Lone wolves sound cool in movies, but in real life, they often end up **lonely wolves.** Midlife is the perfect time to **rebuild old connections, strengthen existing ones, and maybe even make new friends.** Because no one wants to reach their 60s and realize the only "friend" they regularly talk to is their dentist.

So, men—call up an old friend today. Your mental health will thank you.

2. Stress, Anger, and Managing Emotions

Why Men Explode (and Women Express Themselves in 174 Different Ways)

Stress and anger are like uninvited guests at a party—you don't want them there, but they show up anyway, eat all the snacks, and refuse to leave. The difference between men and women? Women tend to **talk about** their stress, analyze it, and find support. Men? Men often **swallow it, suppress it, and then one day, snap because someone left the toilet seat up.**

Let's break this down before someone gets unnecessarily mad at their Wi-Fi speed.

How Stress Works: Men vs. Women

Stress is an unavoidable part of life—bills, work deadlines, family responsibilities, and the existential crisis of "Why did I walk into this room?" all contribute to it. But men and women **process stress differently**, and that difference can be as dramatic as a Bollywood climax.

Women's Stress Response: The "Let's Talk It Out" Method

Stressed Woman: "I need to talk!"

Other Woman: "I'm here! Spill everything!"

"So, first of all, my boss was impossible today, then the dog wouldn't stop barking, and I still haven't finished that project. Also, I feel bloated, I think I'm aging, and do you think I should switch to herbal tea?"

"Oh my God, SAME. Let's discuss in full detail."

One hour, two cups of chai, and several "I totally get you" statements later—stress levels decrease.

Women are biologically wired to handle stress through **connection and communication**. When they feel overwhelmed, their brain releases oxytocin, the **"bonding hormone,"** which encourages them to seek support.

Men's Stress Response: The "Silence and Simmer" Strategy

Stressed Man: (Sits quietly, stares at the ceiling, scrolls through his phone mindlessly.)
Concerned Wife: "Are you okay?"
"I'm fine."
"You don't look fine."
"I said I'm fine."
(Raises an eyebrow, knowing an emotional eruption is approximately 72 hours away.)

Men don't naturally produce as much oxytocin, so their stress response leans toward **"fight or flight."** This means they either:

1. **Get angry** (fight mode)—snapping at the barista because she forgot their extra shot of espresso.

1. **Withdraw completely** (flight mode)—becoming emotionally unavailable, disappearing into work, or suddenly developing an intense interest in watching documentaries about World War II.

Why Anger is a Go-To Emotion for Men

Anger is like a universal **default setting** for many men. It's not because they want to be angry all the time—it's just that **expressing stress, sadness, or vulnerability often feels "unacceptable."**

A man showing stress at work? Seen as weak.

A man saying, "I feel really sad about this"? Met with awkward silence.

A man getting angry? Ah, now that's considered normal behavior.

Society has conditioned men to believe that **anger is strong**, but sadness or stress makes them "less manly." As a result, men internalize everything until one day, they're screaming at a traffic light for turning red too soon.

3. The Health Risks of Unmanaged Stress & Anger

Bottled-up stress isn't just bad for mental health—it's also **a direct highway to health problems.** Chronic stress and unmanaged anger can lead to:

High blood pressure

Increased risk of heart attacks

Sleep problems (yes, stress is why you wake up at 3 AM thinking about an awkward conversation from 10 years ago)

Relationship issues (because "I'm fine" is not an actual explanation)

How to Actually Manage Stress Without Yelling at Your Phone
Men don't need to suddenly turn into meditation gurus or start writing poetry (unless they want to, which is cool). But here are **some realistic ways** to **keep stress in check** before it turns into a full-blown Hulk smash:

Find an outlet – Whether it's exercise, music, or even just yelling at the TV during a game, **let the frustration out in a healthy way.**

Talk—but start small – No one expects a monologue about feelings on day one. But even a "Man, today was rough" is better than radio silence.

Get a hobby that isn't just work – Fixing the garage door doesn't count. Find something enjoyable that helps you relax.

Breathe. No, seriously, breathe. – Stress increases when you forget to **slow down and take deep breaths.** (And no, sighing loudly doesn't count.)

Know when to walk away – If your stress is at explosion level, take a break before reacting. Many an argument could have been avoided if a man just took 10 seconds to breathe before responding with "I don't care where we eat."

Final Thoughts: Stress is Normal, Explosion is Optional

Men, you **don't** have to bottle everything up until you explode over something trivial—like someone using the last of the toothpaste. Stress is inevitable, but **how you handle it is within your control.**

And remember—saying "I'm fine" when you're absolutely not fine is the emotional equivalent of duct-taping a leaking pipe. Sooner or later, **it's going to burst.**

Talk. Laugh. Take a break. And for the love of your mental health—stop fighting with traffic lights.

4. The Pressure to Provide

Why Men Are Still Carrying the World on Their Shoulders

If you ask most men in their 40s what keeps them up at night, you'll probably hear some variation of: *"Bills, mortgage, retirement, college fees, and why my car suddenly makes that weird noise."* The pressure to provide isn't just a societal expectation—it's practically tattooed on every man's brain from birth.

The Unwritten Rule: "Thou Shalt Provide"

From a young age, boys are taught that their worth is tied to their ability to provide. It starts small—helping dad carry the groceries, mowing the lawn, maybe even splitting the bill on a date. But by the time they hit 40, the game has leveled up. Now, it's not just about paying for dinner—it's about keeping the family afloat, planning for retirement, and making sure the fridge never runs out of milk (which, let's be honest, mysteriously disappears faster than common sense at a New year sale).

Meanwhile, society hasn't exactly eased up on these expectations. While gender roles have evolved in many ways, the old-school belief that a *"real man"* provides financially still looms large. Whether a man is the sole earner, a co-provider, or even a stay-at-home dad, the pressure is always there. And if financial struggles hit? Well, that's when the sleepless nights and stress-induced graying accelerate like a bad stock market crash.

The Silent Stress of Money Worries

Let's picture two scenarios.

Scenario One: A man in his 40s gets hit with an unexpected financial setback—maybe a job loss, an investment gone wrong, or an eye-watering college tuition bill for his kid who just switched majors *for the third time.* His response? He doesn't talk about it. Instead, he internalizes the stress, mentally calculates worst-case scenarios, and probably Googles *"How to retire by 50 without selling a kidney."*

Scenario Two: A woman in the same situation? She immediately picks up the phone and calls her sister, her best friend, or even a stranger in line at Starbucks. She vents, gets advice, hears some *"Don't worry, it'll work out"* pep talks, and maybe cries it out. By the end of it, she feels emotionally lighter, while the man in Scenario One is still staring blankly at the ceiling at 2 AM, calculating the cost of living if he moves to a remote village.

The problem isn't just financial strain—it's how men handle it. Unlike women, who often lean on emotional support networks, many men don't feel comfortable sharing their financial fears. Instead, they carry the burden alone, which only adds to stress, anxiety, and those mysterious stomach pains doctors can never quite diagnose.

Gender Roles: Changing, But Not Fast Enough

Now, here's where things get interesting. In many households, women are equal financial contributors. Some even out-earn their husbands. And yet, many men still feel that *deep down*, it's their job to be the provider. Call it cultural conditioning, societal pressure, or just years of watching dads, uncles, and grandfathers do the same thing—but that weight doesn't just disappear.

For some men, accepting a partner's financial contribution feels empowering. For others, it feels like failure (*which, by the way, it's NOT*). The problem isn't who earns more—it's the rigid belief that *a man must always earn more to be valuable.*

Breaking the Cycle: The Key to Mental Well-Being

So, what's the solution? No, it's not suddenly throwing money worries out the window (*although winning the lottery would help*). It's about shifting the mindset:

- **Talk about it:** Financial stress isn't a solo burden. Sharing worries with a spouse, friend, or even a financial advisor can ease the pressure.

- **Redefine success:** Being a provider isn't just about money. It's about being emotionally present, supporting your family in *all* ways, and ensuring *yourself* a good life, too.

- **Ditch the shame:** There is no shame in job loss, career shifts, or financial struggles. It's part of life, and it does *not* define a man's worth.

- **Find balance:** Working 80-hour weeks just to keep up with societal expectations is not a badge of honor—it's a direct path to burnout. It's okay to slow down, reassess, and focus on personal happiness, too.

At the end of the day, men don't have to *carry* the world. They just have to *live* in it—without letting money, stress, and expectations steal their peace.

5. Redefining Masculinity and Purpose

Why It's Time for Men to Reimagine Their Superhero Personas

Let's start with a question: *What makes a man "manly"?* Is it the ability to fix a leaky faucet without calling in the plumber? Or is it how much weight you can lift at the gym without looking like you're about to collapse into a puddle of sweat? Society has long told men that *masculinity* is about strength, stoicism, and emotional restraint. But what if we told you that redefining masculinity could actually make you stronger, happier, and more connected to the world around you?

Let's start by debunking some myths.

Myth 1: "Real Men Don't Cry"

You've probably heard this one. It's the same old, tired advice that suggests crying or showing vulnerability is somehow a sign of weakness. But what if we flipped that on its head? Imagine a man in his 40s, let's call him *Dave*—he's been carrying around the emotional weight of a failed business venture, the stress of a troubled relationship, and the constant fear of *not being enough*. One day, while watching *The Lion King* (don't ask), Dave starts tearing up as Mufasa dies. It's not the cartoon lion that's getting to him—it's all the feelings he's been holding in for years.

Instead of fighting those tears, Dave allows himself to cry. And guess what? That's not weakness—it's *emotional strength*. By giving himself permission to feel, Dave releases pent-up stress and emotional baggage that he didn't even realize he was carrying.

This is where masculinity and vulnerability can co-exist. The men who are truly in touch with their emotional health are the ones who are able to live with purpose, authenticity, and a deeper sense of self.

Myth 2: "Men Don't Need Self-Care"
Now, let's talk about self-care. The phrase *"self-care"* often conjures images of spa days, face masks, and bubble baths. While these might sound wonderful (hello, *sudden* interest in cucumbers on my eyes), the truth is that self-care for men doesn't need to be "girly" or indulgent.

Take Sushant, for example. Sushant is a 42-year-old lawyer who's been pushing himself to the brink for years. Late nights, high-stakes cases, and a seemingly endless stack of paperwork have left him feeling more like a robot than a person. His emotional health? Out the window. Sushant decides to start a simple, 10-minute morning ritual: a few minutes of meditation, some light stretching, and a cup of coffee without his phone in hand. It's not revolutionary, but for the first time in a long time, Sushant feels like he's taking care of himself. He feels energized, more focused at work, and, dare we say, less likely to snap at the cashier for taking too long.

Self-care is a game-changer, and it doesn't need to be complicated. Whether it's a walk in nature, journaling, or just taking time to enjoy a hobby, men need to embrace the fact that taking care of their mental health isn't a luxury—it's a necessity.

How Men Can Learn from Women's Approaches to Purpose

Women have historically been more open to talking about their emotions, mental health, and what brings them joy. The result? Many women in their 40s and beyond have mastered the art of *finding purpose* through personal growth, relationships, and emotional well-being.

Let's look at *Sarah*, a 45-year-old woman who has spent years being "the caretaker." Her career has been successful, her children are grown, and her relationship is solid—but she's realized that her personal purpose has been somewhat neglected. Instead of following the traditional path of "doing it all" for everyone else, Sarah takes a leap and signs up for a pottery class. She's never done it before, but it's something that brings her joy. Through this simple, creative outlet, Sarah reconnects with her sense of self and finds fulfillment in a way she hadn't in years.

So, what can men learn from Sarah's journey? Purpose isn't just about career success or being the breadwinner. It's about connecting with the things that bring you fulfillment, joy, and emotional health. And sometimes, that means doing something for *you*—not just for others.

Building a Support Network

1. How Men Can Build Friendships, Connect with Others, and Not Just Talk About the Weather

Let's be honest for a moment: when was the last time you had a real conversation with your guy friends? You know, the kind where you dive into meaningful topics like *how you're feeling about life*, not just the latest sports game or who's going to win the next round of golf.

For most men, friendships often revolve around doing stuff together—watching football, fishing, or grabbing beers after work. These connections are meaningful in their own right, but what about the deeper, emotional connections that can provide a real support network when life starts throwing curveballs?

In this chapter, we're going to explore how men can go beyond small talk and develop genuine friendships and support systems that help their mental health in ways that watching a game simply can't.

Why Men Struggle to Build Strong Social Connections

Here's the thing: Men, especially in their 40s, often find it difficult to open up about their emotions or vulnerabilities. If you've ever tried talking to your buddy about your mental health or the stress of balancing work and family life, you know it can feel like you're speaking a foreign language. Your friend might nod sympathetically, but all you're really getting back is, "Yeah, man. Work's been rough for me too. So, what's the score of the game tonight?"

This is a bit of a problem. While women typically have no issue forming close-knit emotional circles where they can talk about anything and everything, men often bottle things up or try to navigate their struggles on their own. There's a societal expectation that men should be independent, strong, and self-reliant, which can make it harder to reach out and ask for help when needed.

But here's the kicker—*we all need a support network*. No man is an island, and emotional isolation is a sure-fire way to dive headfirst into a midlife crisis. So how can men build these emotional connections? Let's break it down.

Strategy 1: Go Beyond the "Hey, How's Work?"

It's time to get past the superficial greetings. If you want to form deeper, more meaningful friendships, you need to start asking the real questions. Don't just ask how your friend's job is going—ask how he's really feeling about it. Try asking things like:

"What's been the most challenging part of your week?"

"Have you been doing anything to de-stress lately?"

"What's something you're excited about right now?"

These types of questions show that you care about more than just the surface-level stuff. It can open the door to a conversation that's more than just about work, sports, or cars. It gives your friend the opportunity to share feelings, concerns, or even vulnerabilities that they may not have expressed before. And don't forget to *listen*. When your friend opens up, really hear them. It's not about fixing their problems; it's about showing that you understand and that you're there for them.

Strategy 2: Join Groups That Align With Your Interests

Not all support networks have to be built through one-on-one conversations. Sometimes, the best way to find deeper connections is through group activities. Whether it's joining a sports league, a local volunteer group, or a men's book club, these activities give you a chance to meet new people and form friendships based on common interests.

Take Puneet, for example. Puneet was always a "lone wolf" type, doing everything himself. But one day, he joined a weekend hiking group just to get out of the house and exercise. To his surprise, the hikes didn't just offer physical benefits—they allowed him to meet like-minded men who were also looking for deeper connections. Through hiking and casual chats along the trail, Puneet built lasting friendships where they discussed everything from family dynamics to financial pressures. Now, these hiking trips have become more than just outdoor activities—they're an essential part of his support network.

Strategy 3: Be the One to Reach Out

A common misconception about male friendships is that they always need to be initiated by others. The truth is, *you* can be the one to start reaching out. It doesn't have to be a big gesture—sometimes it's just sending a text to check in on a friend or inviting them to grab a coffee.

Think about Arsh, who noticed that his old college buddy had been quieter than usual. Instead of waiting for his friend to reach out, Arsh decided to send a quick "Hey, you doing okay?" message. It opened the door to a heart-to-heart conversation where his friend admitted he had been struggling with his health and didn't know who to talk to. By being the one to initiate the connection, Arsh created a safe space for his friend to express what he was going through.

Gender Differences in Social Connections: Men vs. Women

While men may struggle to build deeper emotional connections, women, on the other hand, often have an easier time creating rich social networks. Women tend to form friendships that provide emotional support, and they are more likely to seek out help when they're feeling stressed, anxious, or overwhelmed. Women are also more inclined to reach out for regular "check-ins" and maintain a consistent dialogue with their close circle of friends.

For example, *Lina* has a group of girlfriends she's been close with since high school. Every few weeks, they get together for a dinner, where the conversation naturally flows from the lighthearted to the deeply personal. They talk about relationships, health, work, and anything else that's on their minds. This emotional support system not only helps Lina feel validated and heard, but it also fosters a sense of connection and belonging.

Men, however, often wait until they're at a breaking point before they reach out. The difference is that women's social networks often act as a buffer, preventing them from hitting that point in the first place. Men may not realize the value of these support networks until they're struggling to cope with a major life stressor—like a job loss, divorce, or health scare.

2. How Building a Strong Support Network Affects Mental Health

The benefits of having a reliable support network are *huge*. Research shows that men who are more connected to others experience lower levels of anxiety, depression, and stress. They are also better equipped to handle life's challenges, whether it's managing work-life balance or dealing with personal crises.

Having a support system also promotes resilience—the ability to bounce back from adversity. Whether you're venting about work, discussing family dynamics, or simply hanging out, those social connections play a vital role in maintaining your mental well-being.

Hence, men in their 40s can't afford to overlook the importance of building and nurturing friendships. A strong support network doesn't just improve your mental health—it also helps you live a more fulfilling, balanced life. So, next time you're watching the game with your buddies, try slipping in a deeper question or two. Who knows? You might just find a friend who's willing to have an *actual* conversation.

3. Spiritual and Holistic Approaches to Mental Well-Being

The Mind-Body Connection: How stress, anxiety, and emotions affect men's physical health.

Ever seen a man rubbing his temples like he's trying to erase a whiteboard inside his head? That's stress, my friend. It starts as a **tiny worry**, grows into a **full-blown mental hurricane**, and before you know it—**boom!**—your back hurts, your blood pressure is doing the cha-cha, and your hairline is waving you a slow goodbye.

Men often **ignore stress** like they ignore instruction manuals—until things start falling apart. Anxiety? "Nah, just overthinking." Sleep problems? "I'll catch up on the weekend." That nagging pain in the chest? "Probably just gas." (Spoiler alert: It might not be just gas!)

Science proves that **mental stress doesn't just stay in your head**—it sneaks into your **heart, stomach, immune system, and even libido**. Ever heard of the phrase "**worried sick**"? Well, turns out it's **not just a metaphor**. Stress can mess with digestion (hello, acidity!), cause weight gain (or loss), and turn a cheerful man into a grumpy old uncle overnight.

So, gentlemen, if you're feeling like your body is **slowly filing complaints against you**, it's time to **listen up**. Managing your mind isn't just about mental peace—it's about **saving your gut, heart, and that precious remaining hair on your head!**

Ancient Wisdom for Modern Challenges: Applying teachings from Hindu mythology (Bhagavad Gita, Upanishads, Ramayana) to navigate midlife struggles.

Picture this: Arjuna, one of the greatest warriors in history, stands on the battlefield of Kurukshetra—**not ready to fight, but ready to give up**. He's overwhelmed, confused, questioning his purpose. **Sounds familiar?** That's because every man over 40 has his own version of Kurukshetra—whether it's career struggles, financial pressure, relationship conflicts, or just that nagging back pain that won't go away.

But just like Krishna guided Arjuna through **his crisis**, Hindu scriptures offer **timeless wisdom** to help men navigate the battles of midlife.

Lessons from the Bhagavad Gita: Finding Purpose Beyond the Paycheck

Krishna tells Arjuna, **"Do your duty without attachment to the results."**

Translation? **Stop measuring your worth by promotions, bank balance, or society's approval.** True success lies in **effort, not just outcomes.**

Upanishads: Mastering the Mind Over Midlife Chaos

The Upanishads teach: **"You are what your deep, driving desire is."**

By 40, most men are stuck in routines, **losing sight of their inner passions.**

The lesson? **Reconnect with yourself, redefine success, and seek what truly fulfills you.**

Ramayana: Balancing Family & Duty Like Lord Rama

Rama is the **ideal son, husband, and king**—but his life is full of **struggles and sacrifices.**

His story teaches that **no role in life is easy, but grace, patience, and Dharma (duty) guide us through tough times.**

Midlife is about finding that **balance**—between responsibilities and self-care, between duty and personal happiness.

The Modern Kurukshetra: Winning the Battle Within

Life after 40 isn't about just **surviving**—it's about **thriving.** Hindu wisdom doesn't ask men to **run away from challenges**; it teaches how to **face them head-on, with strength, clarity, and inner peace.**

So, whether you're struggling with **work stress, relationships, health, or self-worth,** the answers aren't in Google searches or late-night anxiety sessions. **They've been in our ancient texts all along—waiting to guide you through your own battlefield.**

Meditation & Mantras for Mental Strength: A Cheat Code for Inner Peace

Let's be honest—when someone tells you to meditate, your first thought is: "Who has time for that?" The idea of sitting still, closing your eyes, and "emptying your mind" sounds as impossible as finding a TV remote when you need it. But here's the secret: meditation isn't about doing nothing—it's about doing everything better.

Men over 40 face a mental traffic jam—work stress, family responsibilities, financial worries, health concerns—all buzzing around in their heads like a WhatsApp group that never stops pinging. That's where meditation and mantras come in. Think of them as a reset button for your brain, a way to clear the mental clutter and focus on what truly matters.

Meditation: The Art of Not Losing Your Mind

You don't need to become a Himalayan monk—just five to ten minutes a day can make a difference. Here's how:

1. **Breathe Like a Boss:** Take slow, deep breaths—inhale for four counts, hold for four, exhale for four. Do this five times, and boom—your mind is already calmer.

2. **Body Scan (Without a Doctor's Bill):** Close your eyes and notice how your body feels—where there's tension, stress, or stiffness. Just being aware helps release the tightness.

3. **Thought Traffic Control:** Thoughts will come and go. Don't fight them—just observe them and let them pass. Like a bouncer at a VIP club, allow only the good thoughts in.

Mantras: Ancient Sound Therapy for the Modern Mind

A mantra isn't just a set of fancy Sanskrit words—it's a mental shield against stress and negativity. The vibration of these sounds calms the nervous system and boosts confidence, focus, and inner peace.

Here are some easy, powerful mantras you can chant:

Om Namah Shivaya – For inner strength and resilience

Gayatri Mantra – To sharpen the mind and attract positivity

So Hum – A simple breath mantra meaning "I am that"—a reminder of your own strength

The Real-World Benefits: Why Bother?

Less Stress, More Focus: Helps you think clearly without panic.

Better Sleep, No More Sheep Counting: Calms the nervous system.

Stronger Willpower: You'll handle conflicts and challenges without losing your cool.

Happier Mood: Because a calm man is a wise man.

Final Thought: Meditation & Mantras—Your Mind's Best Gym
Most men work out to keep their body fit—why not train the mind too? Meditation and mantra chanting are like push-ups for your brain—strengthening focus, patience, and emotional balance. And the best part? No gym membership required!

4. The Role of Bhakti (Devotion) and Surrender

Understanding how faith and spirituality can reduce stress and emotional burdens.

Imagine this: You're a man in your 40s, juggling work deadlines, family responsibilities, financial pressures, and that mysterious back pain that appeared out of nowhere.

You've spent your whole life trying to control everything—your career, your relationships, even your emotions. But what if the secret to real peace isn't in controlling life, but in surrendering to something higher?

That's where Bhakti (devotion) and surrender come in. No, this isn't about quitting your job to sit in a temple or turning into a full-time monk. Bhakti is simply shifting the burden of life's struggles onto a higher power—letting go of what you can't control and trusting that everything will fall into place.

Why Devotion is a Stress Buster

Men are taught from childhood that they must be strong, logical, and always in control. But let's face it—life doesn't always go as planned. Promotions don't come when expected, relationships get complicated, health throws surprises, and the stock market has a mind of its own. Trying to control everything is like holding sand—the tighter you grip, the more it slips away.

Bhakti teaches us:

You're not alone. There's a divine force supporting you. When you can't handle the weight of your worries, surrender them.

Faith reduces fear. When you trust in a higher power, anxiety over the future fades. Faith is knowing that even if the path isn't clear, you will be guided.

Devotion brings emotional stability. Whether it's chanting, prayer, or simply sitting in quiet gratitude, faith gives the mind a much-needed reset button.

How to Practice Bhakti in Daily Life

1. **Start the Day with Gratitude:** Instead of waking up and checking your emails, spend two minutes thanking the Divine for what you have—your health, family, and even the challenges that help you grow.

2. **Mantra Chanting for Mental Peace:** Simple chants like "Om Namo Bhagavate Vasudevaya" or "Shree Ram Jai Ram Jai Jai Ram" help silence mental chaos.

3. **Let Go of What You Can't Control:** Worried about finances, job security, or family conflicts? Surrender it to the Divine and focus on what you can do instead.

4. **Read or Listen to Spiritual Wisdom:** Whether it's Bhagavad Gita, Ramayana, or even listening to devotional music, these small acts help cultivate faith.

5. **Trust the Process:** Everything happens for a reason. Bhakti isn't about getting what you want—it's about trusting that you will get what you need.

Surrender is Strength, Not Weakness

Surrender doesn't mean giving up—it means accepting that you don't have to fight every battle alone. When Arjuna was lost in self-doubt, Krishna told him, "Surrender unto me, and I will guide you." This wasn't weakness—it was wisdom.

So, the next time life feels overwhelming, instead of overthinking, overworking, or over-stressing—try Bhakti. Because sometimes, the strongest thing a man can do is let go and trust.

Nature and Pranayama (Breathwork): Using breathing techniques like Anulom Vilom and Bhramari to manage stress and anger.

Let's face it: Life comes at you fast. From work emails pinging like a game of Whack-a-Mole to family responsibilities that make you feel like you're juggling flaming torches, stress is inevitable. And if that's not enough, anger can sneak in, boiling over when least expected. But what if the answer to your stress and anger was hiding in the most basic thing you do every day? Yes, we're talking about breathing.

We all breathe, right? But do we really *breathe*? Here's a fun fact: The way we breathe directly impacts our physical and mental health. Deep, controlled breathing is the antidote to the mental traffic jam we often experience in our busy lives. And that's where pranayama (breathwork) comes in.

What is Pranayama?

Pranayama is an ancient practice from yoga that focuses on controlling the breath. It's like the "Ctrl + Alt + Del" for your brain. Through specific breathing techniques, pranayama helps you calm the mind, reduce stress, and balance your emotions. Think of it as mental yoga. And here's a simple truth: If you're a man over 40, you can't afford to ignore your breath.

5. Top Breathing Techniques to Keep Your Cool

1. Anulom Vilom (Nadi Shodhana): The Balancer of the Mind

This technique involves alternating nostrils while breathing, and it's like hitting the reset button for your mind.

How to do it:
Sit comfortably with your spine straight.

Place your right thumb on your right nostril and inhale deeply through the left nostril.

Close the left nostril with your right ring finger and exhale through the right nostril.

Repeat this cycle for 5 to 10 minutes.

Why it works: Anulom Vilom helps balance the left and right hemispheres of the brain and reduces stress by calming the nervous system. It's like giving your mind a mini vacation while you're still sitting at your desk.

2. Bhramari (Bee Breath): The Stress-Zapper

When stress and anger are building up like a pressure cooker, Bhramari is your valve to release the steam. It's as simple as humming. No, seriously—humming like you're a bee can do wonders for your mental health.

How to do it:
Sit in a quiet place and close your eyes.

Inhale deeply and as you exhale, make a loud humming sound (like the sound of a bee).

Focus on the vibration you feel in your head.

Repeat this for 5 to 10 minutes.

Why it works: Bhramari has an immediate calming effect. The humming sound stimulates the vagus nerve, which is responsible for regulating your stress response. This technique is like hitting the mental mute button—no more anger, no more anxiety, just peace.

3. Ujjayi Pranayama: The Victory Breath

Also known as the "Ocean Breath," this technique is a gentle way to create a sense of inner calm while still feeling energized.

How to do it:
Sit comfortably and inhale deeply through your nose.

As you exhale, create a sound similar to the ocean (like a soft "ha" sound) by constricting your throat slightly.

Breathe slowly and deeply, maintaining the ocean-like sound.

Why it works: Ujjayi helps increase oxygen supply to the brain and enhances mental clarity. It's great for calming the mind while still keeping you alert and focused—perfect for when you need to handle stress, but don't want to feel lethargic.

Why Breathwork is a Game-Changer for Men Over 40

As men age, stressors tend to multiply—career challenges, family dynamics, health issues—and all of this can impact both your mental and physical well-being. Pranayama helps:

Reduce stress and anxiety—It calms the nervous system by slowing the heart rate.

Improve mental clarity—Breathing deeply boosts oxygen levels to the brain, which improves focus and decision-making.

Relieve anger and frustration—Breathing deeply is like giving your anger and stress a timeout.

Boost physical health—Breathing exercises help **with** blood circulation, and lung capacity, and can even lower blood pressure.

So: Breathe, and Let It Be

CHAPTER SIX

The Silent Battle with the Mirror

1. The Silent Impact of Physical Appearance & Aging on Men

Let's be honest—aging is unfair. One day, you're a young, confident man, and the next, you're squinting at your reflection, wondering when your hairline started resembling a receding tide. Unlike women, who openly discuss every wrinkle, every gray hair, and every possible anti-aging solution in their WhatsApp groups, men mostly suffer in silence.

But here's the truth—aging hits men just as hard, even if they don't admit it. That first gray hair in the beard? It's not "distinguished." It's a betrayal. The sudden discovery that metabolism has packed its bags and left for a permanent vacation? A cruel joke. And let's not even talk about the belly—because, apparently, it's the one thing that's *thriving* in midlife.

The Bald Truth About Hair Loss

Ah, the classic male struggle—**hair loss.** While women have hair spa treatments, volumizing sprays, and extensions, men have

denial. First, they pretend it's just the way the light is hitting their scalp. Then, they switch to hats. Eventually, they make the brave decision to go full Vin Diesel and embrace baldness. **(Respect to the men who accept fate without comb overs!)**

But here's the thing—**hair loss isn't just about looks; it messes with confidence.** Some men feel they start blending into the background, that they no longer look as powerful, youthful, or attractive. Society doesn't make it any easier—bald men are either expected to go the **"macho Bruce Willis"** route or the **"dad who gave up"** path.

The Great Metabolism Betrayal

Remember the good old days when you could eat an entire pizza and wake up with **abs?** Yeah, those days are **gone.** Somewhere around 40, your body decides that **everything you eat should now be stored for future emergencies.** You eat a slice of cake? Congratulations, you've just committed to a month of extra belly fat.

The worst part? **Women seem to have an entire ecosystem of diet plans, fitness groups, and detox regimens.** Meanwhile, men are left wondering why their old workout routine from college stopped working. Spoiler alert: It's because metabolism is **on strike.**

The Wrinkle Epidemic

Men don't really care about wrinkles until one day, they wake up, glance at their reflection, and wonder, **"Since when did I look permanently exhausted?"** The forehead lines, crow's feet, and sagging jawline are all **subtle reminders that time is moving faster than we'd like.**

Women have night creams, eye serums, and botox appointments. Men? They **splash water on their face and hope for the best.**

So What Can Men Do?

Here's the good news—aging doesn't mean **declining.** It just means **adapting.** If women can dedicate entire sections of their lives to anti-aging strategies, men can at least put in some effort.

Exercise matters – A little strength training and cardio can do wonders, not just for the body but for confidence.

Eat like you care – No, you don't have to live on kale, but maybe stop treating your stomach like a garbage disposal.

Skincare isn't just for women – A decent moisturizer and sunscreen won't take away your masculinity. (In fact, it'll take away **five years off your face.**)

Mindset is everything – If you carry yourself with confidence, people won't notice the wrinkles—they'll notice the presence. **Mature like a fine whisky, not like expired milk.**

The bottom line? **You're not alone in this.** Every man in his 40s is secretly mourning his youth in the bathroom mirror. The trick is to **Here are some helpful perspective, self-compassion, and practical tips for men dealing with the effects of aging.Age is a Mindset, Not Just a Number:**

Yes, you may notice a few more gray hairs or an extra layer around your midsection, but aging is about how you feel, not just how you look. Take control of your health, your habits, and your mindset. If you decide you're still in your prime, the world will follow suit. Confidence is timeless.

Embrace What You Can't Control, Change What You Can

Some things are just inevitable, like wrinkles and hair loss, but you can still control your fitness, health, and overall vitality. Focus on what's in your power—regular exercise, healthy eating, and staying active mentally. You may not reverse time, but you can feel great at any age.

Stop Taking Yourself Too Seriously

Sure, your younger self may have had a six-pack and a full head of hair, but don't let nostalgia make you miserable. Instead, laugh about it. Humor is the best anti-aging solution. The more you laugh at the changes, the less they'll bother you.

The Bald Look is Not a Setback, It's a New Look

Many men fear baldness, but the reality is, a shaved head is not a "giving up" signal—it's a style choice. Embrace it like the cool, confident guy you are, and get some head care products to make your scalp shine like it's a runway.

Emotional Health Matters, Too

It's okay to be vulnerable. Aging often brings up existential questions and fears about the future. It's essential to open up, talk, and connect with others. Embrace the importance of emotional well-being as much as physical health.

Invest in Your Self-Care Like You Would a Business

Just as you'd put time, energy, and money into a successful business venture, invest in yourself. This could mean hiring a personal trainer, attending therapy, or even learning to relax. It's not selfish—it's necessary for long-term happiness.

Comparison is the Thief of Joy

Don't compare yourself to younger guys or the "fit-for-life" 40-year-olds you see on social media. Your journey is unique. Aging may slow things down physically, but it brings wisdom, experience, and a deeper understanding of what matters. Own it.

2. The silent impact of physical appearance and aging on women

Aging for women comes with its own set of unique experiences, but let's face it, ladies—society has a strange love-hate relationship with aging women. One minute, we're expected to look forever youthful, and the next, we're being told to embrace our wisdom and "let go" of our youthful appearance. The pressure? Absolutely real. The truth? Aging is a beautiful, nuanced journey—and it's time to take ownership of that.

From wrinkles and gray hairs to newfound confidence and self-acceptance, aging brings a whole new set of challenges. But here's the truth: aging is just another chapter of your story.

Aging and the Mirror:

Much like men, the mirror can become a source of silent battles. Those laugh lines? A sign of joy-filled years (unless you're just realizing your makeup has settled into those lines—then, that's a "whoops" moment!). And those grays? They are **wisdom highlights**, because, let's face it, every gray hair tells a story—whether you're ready to share it or not. The real trick is accepting that **aging doesn't take away your beauty; it deepens it.**

Hormones: A Wild Ride:

If you thought being a teenager was tough, welcome to the hormone roller coaster of perimenopause and menopause! **Hot flashes, night sweats, and mood swings** become part of the daily routine. But there's something liberating about letting go of the monthly struggle and stepping into the power of knowing your body better than ever. Plus, your hair might finally stop fighting gravity. Silver linings, right?

The Silent Strength:

The cultural expectation that women should maintain a "youthful" appearance can be exhausting, but here's where it gets liberating: **Age is the one thing you'll never be able to fake.** The grace and strength that comes with age is something you carry proudly, no longer defined by the number on your birth certificate.

Embracing Your Changing Body:

As the body changes, so too does the understanding of what it means to take care of yourself. What worked in your 20s may not be as effective in your 40s or beyond, but that doesn't mean you're on the decline. It means you're **upgrading**—finding new ways to nourish your body, mind, and soul.

CHAPTER SEVEN

Mindfulness and Inner Peace

1. Finding Your Zen (Without Needing to Be a Yoga Guru)

When you think of mindfulness, what's the first thing that comes to mind? Is it an image of a calm, zen-like person sitting cross-legged on a mountain top, chanting "Om" while surrounded by nature? If you're imagining a peaceful yogi in perfect harmony with the universe—don't worry, you're not alone.

But here's the reality: mindfulness doesn't require you to shave your head or retreat to a monastery. It's not about transforming into a guru. It's simply about finding *a few moments of calm* in a world that's constantly spinning faster than a treadmill set to the highest speed.

In this chapter, we're going to explore how mindfulness can be a game-changer for men looking to manage stress, find a sense of inner peace, and discover more fulfillment—without the need to master any "advanced" meditation techniques.

The Stress Struggle: Men vs. Women

Let's face it: men have stress just like everyone else. But here's the catch: Men *often deal with it in silence.* While women are more likely to reach out to their friends or loved ones when life gets overwhelming, men are typically less inclined to talk about it. Instead, they bottle up their frustrations, shove them down deep, and keep plugging away.

This can lead to a buildup of stress that's as messy as a clogged sink—eventually, it all comes spilling out in ways we don't even realize. Whether it's a short temper, a growing sense of frustration, or physical symptoms like back pain or sleep issues, stress can take a serious toll if we don't have a healthy way to manage it.

Here's where mindfulness comes in. Mindfulness helps us break free from that constant pressure to keep going, to keep "doing." Instead of focusing on all the tasks and deadlines (or stressing about the *1000* emails piling up), mindfulness teaches us to focus on the present moment. It's about slowing down, taking a deep breath, and simply *being.*

Why Mindfulness Works for Men

Mindfulness is particularly effective for men because it offers a simple, no-frills approach to managing stress. There's no need to sit in a lotus position for hours on end (unless you really want to), and there's no requirement to be an expert in zen philosophy. Mindfulness can be as basic as just taking a few minutes a day to check in with yourself, calm your mind, and center your thoughts.

Take *Rishi* for example. He was always the guy who tried to power through life's challenges—whether it was work pressure, family stress, or the endless to-do list. He never made time for himself and kept pushing harder, until one day, he hit a wall. Feeling overwhelmed and exhausted, Rishi decided to give mindfulness a try. At first, he was skeptical—how could sitting quietly for a few minutes really help? But after just a few weeks of practicing deep breathing and being present in the moment, he noticed a huge difference. His stress levels dropped, his sleep improved, and he started feeling more focused. He wasn't trying to fix everything all at once—he was simply learning to be more in control of his thoughts and reactions.

Types of Mindfulness Practices Men Can Try

If you're new to mindfulness, it's totally fine—there's no need to jump straight into full-on meditation. Start small and see what works best for you. Here are a few mindfulness practices that can help men manage stress and find inner peace:

Breathing Exercises

Sometimes, the best way to calm your mind is to focus on your breath. A simple breathing exercise, such as inhaling deeply for a count of four, holding for four, and exhaling for four, can help reset your nervous system and clear your mind. It's a quick and easy way to get a little peace of mind without needing a 90-minute session.

Body Scan Meditation

For men who are more action-oriented, a body scan meditation can be a great way to connect with your body and find inner calm. In this practice, you mentally check in with each part of your body, starting from your toes and working your way up to your head. It's a great way to relax any areas of tension and become more in tune with your physical self.

Mindful Walking

If sitting still feels like torture, try mindful walking. All it takes is a quiet stroll—whether around the block or through a park—where you focus on your movements, your breath, and the sensations in your body. Leave your phone at home, and let your mind focus on *just walking*. It's simple, effective, and gives you a break from the chaos.

Journaling

If you've ever been tempted to just *vent* about your day, journaling can be a great outlet for your thoughts. Write about your frustrations, your goals, and your wins—whatever is on your mind. Not only does this help you organize your thoughts, but it also allows you to reflect on your emotional state and find clarity. Plus, it's much cheaper than therapy (but still incredibly effective).

The Gender Gap in Mindfulness Practices

While mindfulness is a powerful tool for everyone, research suggests that women tend to be more open to mindfulness practices than men. Women often create a supportive network to practice mindfulness together—whether through yoga classes, guided meditations, or book clubs about self-care. Men, on the other hand, might be more hesitant to try these things or feel like it's not "manly" enough.

That said, mindfulness practices can be just as beneficial for men as they are for women. The key is finding the type of mindfulness that resonates with you. For some men, yoga or guided meditation might feel a bit too "out there," but others may find it incredibly effective. The trick is to try different things and see what works best—there's no one-size-fits-all.

The Bottom Line: Mindfulness Equals Mental Health

Men often feel the pressure to be the strong, silent type, to power through life's challenges without ever showing weakness. But practicing mindfulness doesn't make you weak—it makes you stronger. It gives you the tools to handle stress, process emotions, and find a sense of peace in a chaotic world.

So, whether it's taking five minutes to breathe, going for a mindful walk, or journaling about your day, remember that mindfulness isn't about being perfect—it's about being present. It's about taking control of your mental health in a way that works for you, without needing to fit into anyone else's idea of what "wellness" should look like."

And hey, if mindfulness helps you finally find that inner peace, maybe it's worth ditching the old "I'll just power through" attitude. It might even make your *next* conversation about the weather feel a little more interesting.

2. Seeking Help Without Stigma

How to Ask for Help Without Feeling Like a Failure (Spoiler: It's Not Weakness)

Let's be honest—when it comes to asking for help, many men treat it like a four-letter word. Whether it's asking for directions, admitting they don't know how to assemble IKEA furniture, or—heaven forbid—talking about their mental health, men often feel the weight of *"I've got this"* in a way that's not always beneficial.

We've all heard the phrase *"Real men don't ask for help."* But let's pause for a moment: If that were true, then why do some of the strongest, most successful men in the world have personal coaches, therapists, and support systems? It turns out, asking for help is one of the most powerful things you can do for your mental well-being. It's not a sign of weakness—it's a sign of strength.

In this chapter, we'll talk about why seeking help is crucial for men's mental health, how to overcome the stigma that often surrounds it, and the benefits of reaching out for support—whether through therapy, coaching, or support groups. Let's break it down, one step at a time.

The "Tough Guy" Myth: Breaking the Silence

For generations, men have been conditioned to think that seeking help for mental health issues is somehow *unmanly*. We're told to suck it up, keep our emotions in check, and "man up" when life gets tough. As a result, many men struggle in silence, thinking that asking for help will make them appear weak, vulnerable, or incapable. But here's the truth: *Not asking for help is actually what makes you weak.*

Take Piyush, for example. Piyush had been dealing with stress, anxiety, and sleepless nights for years but never thought to talk to anyone about it. He convinced himself that he just needed to power through, that it was a "phase," or that it wasn't that big of a deal. But the more he ignored it, the worse it got. His relationships were strained, he couldn't focus at work, and his physical health started to decline.

One day, after a particularly rough day at work, Piyush finally cracked. He reached out to a friend who suggested he see a therapist. It felt like a big leap for him—what would people think? Would he be labeled as "weak"? But after just a few sessions, Piyush realized something important: asking for help didn't make him weak; it made him stronger. It gave him the tools to manage his stress, take better care of his mental health, and rebuild his life.

The Stigma Around Mental Health for Men

It's no secret that men often face more stigma when it comes to mental health. Society has conditioned men to hide their struggles, bottle up their emotions, and avoid showing vulnerability. But ignoring mental health is like ignoring the "check engine" light in your car—it's only going to lead to bigger problems down the road.

For many men, seeking help feels like admitting failure. They think, *"I'm supposed to have it all together. I'm supposed to be the provider, the protector, the strong one."* But the truth is, mental health doesn't follow a checklist of what makes you "manly." It's a universal need. Whether you're a CEO, a father, a partner, or a friend, you deserve the same mental health support as anyone else.

3. Including the topic of divorce trauma is crucial

As it's a significant issue that many men face in midlife, and it brings unique challenges to their mental health. Men and women may experience divorce differently, especially in their 40s, when they are dealing with the added complexities of children, finances, and self-identity.

Divorce Trauma: The Silent Struggle of Men

Divorce is traumatic for anyone, but for many men in their 40s, it can feel like a breaking point in life—a moment when everything they've worked for, believed in, and strived toward suddenly crumbles. Men don't always have the luxury of talking openly about it, and this silence can lead to deeper, more prolonged emotional struggles. The stigma surrounding men and emotional vulnerability only exacerbates their pain, often leaving them isolated and misunderstood.

Let's understand this with some true stories and interviews:

Story 1: "The Sudden Isolation"

Mitesh was 42 when his wife of 15 years asked for a divorce. He was blindsided—he'd thought everything was fine, that they had a good life, two kids, a stable job. He worked long hours and always made sure his family was provided for. He didn't expect the emotional distance that had crept in over the years to come to a head like this.

When the divorce happened, Mitesh wasn't prepared for the emotional isolation he'd feel. His friends—those he had once shared everything with—seemed to pull away, not knowing how to act around him. His work colleagues started treating him differently, as if his value had diminished because his marriage had ended. The worst part? His children were caught in the middle. While he fought for joint custody, he felt like he was losing them bit by bit, as they began to grow closer to their mother and more distant from him.

Mitesh's story is not unique. Men often face the painful truth that divorce doesn't just end the relationship—it disrupts their social circles, alters the way they're perceived, and impacts their identity as fathers. The societal expectation that men should "move on" quickly or that they should be "tough" and not show weakness only adds to the pressure. What's left behind is a man who feels as if he's carrying the weight of the world in silence.

Story 2: "The Financial Burden"

Mark, 48, had been married for 20 years when he and his wife decided to part ways. They had built a life together—home, savings, and dreams of retirement—but those dreams now seemed shattered. The financial strain of the divorce hit him harder than he ever imagined. He didn't just have to divide his assets, but he also had to maintain two households. The child support, alimony, and legal fees drained his finances. Suddenly, he went from being the provider to feeling as if he was struggling just to keep his head above water.

While women also face financial challenges in divorce, the stigma around men and their role as providers adds an extra layer of pressure. For men like Mark, the loss of financial stability is not just a practical concern—it strikes at their very identity. Society often equates a man's worth with his ability to provide, and when that gets shaken, the emotional toll is immense. Mark's self-worth took a hit that no one seemed to acknowledge, and he found himself unable to talk about his feelings for fear of being judged as weak or incapable.

Story 3: "The Loss of Family"

Brij had been married for 18 years when his wife decided to end their relationship. For him, the hardest part wasn't just the relationship's collapse—it was the loss of the family unit. Every weekend he now spent in an empty house, while his children were with their mother. He missed out on birthdays, holidays, and day-to-day moments that he had once taken for granted. The loneliness that followed wasn't just about missing his wife—it was about missing the family he had built and the role he had played in it.

What Brij faced—losing access to the daily lives of his children—is something that men experience far more often than women after divorce. For many men, especially those in their 40s, their identity has been so intertwined with being a father and a provider that losing access to their children can feel like losing a part of themselves. The emotional toll is immense, and it's a struggle that doesn't always get the attention it deserves. Women are often more likely to retain the primary caregiving role, leaving men to grapple with feelings of abandonment, guilt, and powerlessness.

4. The Hidden Struggles: What Men Face Post-Divorce

1. **Social Stigma and Judgment**: Men going through a divorce often face social judgment, whether it's from friends, family, or even coworkers. In many cases, they are viewed as less capable or as failures, especially if their marriage falls apart in midlife. The stigma around divorce often feels heavier for men, who are expected to "suck it up" and keep moving forward.

2. **Emotional Support Networks**: While women tend to lean on friends, family, and communities for emotional support during and after divorce, men often retreat into isolation. This lack of a built-in support system exacerbates their emotional pain. In many cases, men find it difficult to express their feelings or seek help, because society has conditioned them to suppress vulnerability.

3. **The Battle for Custody**: In divorce cases, men often find themselves fighting harder for custody of their children. While there's been progress in equalizing parental rights, many men still face an uphill battle when it comes to securing shared custody or being able to maintain an active role in their children's lives. This loss of connection with their children can lead to profound feelings of sadness, anger, and powerlessness.

4. **Changes in Identity and Purpose**: The end of a marriage often forces men to question their identity. They may have defined themselves by their roles as husbands and fathers, and now, without those roles, they struggle to find a sense of purpose. The pressure to redefine oneself in midlife can be overwhelming, especially when the tools and support to help with this transition aren't readily available.

Divorce: The Unseen Struggles

Divorce can be an overwhelming experience, not just emotionally, but financially and mentally as well. The burden of providing alimony or hefty settlements can push many men into a corner. Unfortunately, the pressure is so immense for some that they feel they have no way out. It's a harsh reality, but there are numerous unreported cases where men, feeling unable to meet these financial demands, tragically succumb to the weight of their circumstances. The toll on their mental health can be unbearable—leading to extreme decisions like suicide, simply because they cannot provide the required alimony or settle debts. This is a silent crisis that often goes unnoticed, as the stigma around mental health and seeking help prevents these men from reaching out.

A call for change now

In the modern world, where gender equality is a key focus, it's essential to recognize that support systems should extend equally to both men and women. While there are numerous NGOs and organizations dedicated to the empowerment and well-being of women, particularly during challenging times like divorce, there is a noticeable gap when it comes to providing similar support for men. Unfortunately, many men, especially those navigating the complexities of divorce, find themselves without adequate resources or guidance.

While women have access to various forms of support, legal or emotional, men often feel isolated in their struggles. In certain cases, laws designed to protect women have been misused, and some women take undue advantage of these protections, causing harm and emotional distress to their partners. This not only contributes to the trauma of divorce but also perpetuates the idea that men do not deserve the same level of support in times of crisis.

For true gender equality to be realized, it's essential that society recognizes the mental, emotional, and financial challenges men face, particularly in situations like divorce. The creation of support groups, legal reforms, and counseling services specifically tailored to men in distress is crucial. It is time for the world to address this imbalance and create spaces where men can find support, healing, and a sense of community, just as women have long been able to.

CHAPTER EIGHT

Moving Forward: Rebuilding After Divorce

1. Comparing How Men and Women Seek Help

It's clear that men face unique challenges in the wake of a divorce. The loss of a relationship, children, finances, and social status can leave deep scars. However, acknowledging these struggles and seeking help is the first step toward healing. It's important for men to build new support networks, whether through therapy, support groups, or new friendships. It's also crucial to find ways to express their emotions and re-establish a sense of self-worth beyond their roles as providers or husbands.

Divorce doesn't define a man—it's simply another chapter in the story of who he is. With time, support, and self-compassion, he can emerge from this chapter stronger, more self-aware, and more capable of finding fulfillment in the next phase of life.

This section emphasizes that while divorce trauma is often seen from a gender-neutral perspective, the specific issues men face post-divorce—emotional isolation, financial strain, and identity shifts—can have long-lasting effects on their mental health. Addressing these struggles with compassion, while offering practical ways for men to rebuild, is essential for their overall well-being.

Men and women often approach mental health help in different ways, and that's okay. While women are generally more open about discussing their feelings and seeking therapy or counseling, men tend to be more hesitant.

Women tend to have emotional support networks—friends, family, or online communities—where they openly talk about their struggles, share advice, and encourage each other to seek help. These support systems create a sense of solidarity and make it easier to talk about things like anxiety, depression, or relationship issues.

Men, on the other hand, often struggle with opening up. A man might think, *"I'll just deal with this on my own. I don't want to burden anyone with my problems."* This reluctance can be a barrier to getting help, leaving men feeling isolated and unsupported.

But here's the catch: the more men hide their struggles, the harder it becomes to break the cycle. Men can often feel like they're the only ones dealing with stress, anxiety, or depression—when, in fact, they're not alone at all. There are other men facing the same challenges. And there are therapists, coaches, and support groups specifically designed to help men navigate these issues.

The Benefits of Therapy, Coaching, and Support Groups

Seeking help can come in many forms: therapy, coaching, or support groups. Each has its own set of benefits, and it's important to find what works best for you.

Therapy offers a safe, confidential space where you can talk about your thoughts and feelings without judgment. A therapist can help you develop coping strategies, gain insight into your mental health, and explore deeper emotional issues. Therapy isn't just for "broken" people—it's for anyone who wants to understand themselves better and live a more fulfilled life.

Coaching is more goal-oriented and action-focused. A coach can help you clarify your goals, overcome obstacles, and build a roadmap for your life. Coaching is ideal for men who want to take a proactive approach to personal growth and find solutions to specific challenges they're facing.

Support Groups provide a sense of community and camaraderie. These groups bring together people who are going through similar struggles, allowing them to share experiences, advice, and encouragement. Whether it's a group for men dealing with anxiety, stress, or divorce, support groups create a safe space where men can open up and feel understood.

Overcoming the Stigma

Here's the thing: no one's perfect. We all need help at some point, and there's no shame in asking for it. If anything, reaching out for help is one of the bravest things a person can do. It shows that you recognize the importance of your mental health and that you're willing to take action to improve it.

So, if you're struggling, don't be afraid to ask for help. Talk to a friend, a therapist, or even a coach. Seek out a support group. And remember, asking for help is not a sign of weakness—it's a sign of strength.

To all the men out there—your mental health matters. It's time to let go of the stigma, break the silence, and start taking care of your mind, body, and spirit. Because, in the end, the best way to be strong is to be honest with yourself—and there's nothing weak about that. Men also have layers - more like onions versus rose petals.

2. Daily Routines for Mental Well-Being

How to Start Your Day Without Feeling Like You Need a Nap by 9 AM

We've all heard it before: "Morning routines are the key to success." But let's be real—sometimes getting out of bed is the hardest part of the day. The mental fog, the *"I'll just check my emails for five minutes"* that somehow turns into a full hour of scrolling through cat memes, and the struggle to get a single cup of coffee that doesn't taste like it was brewed by a sleep-deprived raccoon. It's no wonder men often feel like their mental health is a bit off-track.

But here's the thing: it doesn't have to be that way. Crafting a daily routine for mental well-being doesn't mean you need to wake up at 4 AM to meditate while eating kale and listening to a podcast about the benefits of cold showers.

You don't have to be *that* guy. However, adding some simple, intentional habits to your day can significantly improve your mental health, boost your productivity, and help you feel more centered.

In this chapter, we're going to break down some daily routines that are both practical and effective for men. Plus, we'll explore the routines women often use and figure out how to adapt them to fit men's needs (because let's face it—no man wants to do 30 minutes of "gentle yoga" in the living room while wearing an aromatherapy diffuser).

Start Your Day Like You Actually Want to Be Awake

Here's a secret—how you start your morning sets the tone for the rest of your day. But here's the kicker: you don't need to be a superhuman with a checklist of twenty-five things to do before 6 AM to be successful.

Simple steps for a morning routine that doesn't suck:

1. **Wake up and hydrate**: Water is your friend. I don't care if it's the first thing you do or the second (after hitting snooze three times), but drink some water. Your brain is 75% water, and it's doing a terrible job of working when you're walking around in dehydration mode.

2. **Move your body**: You don't need to run a marathon or do 50 pushups. A 10-minute stretch or a brisk walk outside gets your blood flowing and sets a positive tone for the day. Plus, it'll stop your back from feeling like you just did battle with your mattress.

3. **Have a "mindful moment"**: Don't panic—we're not talking about an hour-long meditation retreat. Start small. Take a few minutes to check in with yourself. Breathe deeply, think about something you're grateful for, or simply reflect on how you're feeling. This can help ground you before the rush of emails, meetings, and whatever else life throws your way.

4. **Breakfast of champions**: You know that saying about how breakfast is the most important meal of the day? Well, it's true. But no one said it had to be a salad with quinoa. A simple, healthy breakfast (think oatmeal, eggs, or a smoothie) will fuel you up and keep you energized.

Building a Routine That Actually Sticks

Consistency is key when it comes to mental well-being, but here's the thing: routines need to be realistic. Don't set yourself up to fail by planning a daily routine that's more complicated than assembling IKEA furniture. Start small and build it over time.

Simple Daily Routines for Mental Health

1. **Set time for reflection**: We all have moments where our thoughts run wild, and it's hard to focus. But taking 10 minutes at the end of the day to reflect on your emotions can help process them. You don't have to do it by journaling in a leather-bound book like a 19th-century poet, either. Simply think about the highs and lows of your day, and what you can learn from them.

2. **Move it or lose it**: Physical activity is not only good for your body; it's essential for your mental health. Aim for at least 30 minutes of activity, whether it's a brisk walk, a weight session, or even hitting the gym. But remember—don't treat this as punishment for eating a donut. It's about feeling good and giving your mind a boost.

3. **Connect with someone**: Relationships are a huge part of mental wellness, so make time to reach out to someone you trust—whether that's a friend, a partner, or even a colleague. Just chatting about something non-work related can lift your spirits and strengthen your support system.

4. **Set boundaries**: This is where we get real—burnout is a serious thing. Make time for yourself by learning to say no to things that drain your energy. Set clear boundaries between work and

personal life, and respect your own space. This is one area where you'll want to channel your inner superhero and put yourself first (because if you're not at your best, you can't be there for others).

3. Women's Routines: What Can We Learn?

It's no secret that women tend to be a little better at keeping up with their mental health routines. But before you get jealous of their "spa nights" and "mindful journaling," let's look at what men can learn from women's routines.

1. **Emotional check-ins**: Women are often more in touch with their emotions, and they make a habit of checking in with themselves regularly. This doesn't have to involve sitting on a therapist's couch for hours—sometimes, it's simply sitting down and thinking about how you feel. Men can learn a lot from this practice of self-reflection, even if it's just five minutes before bed.

2. **Social support**: Women are great at building strong emotional support networks. They're more likely to have close friends they talk to regularly about their feelings. Men, on the other hand, often keep things to themselves. Building deeper friendships and support networks can significantly improve a man's mental well-being.

3. **Self-care isn't selfish**: Women tend to prioritize self-care, whether it's taking time for a bath, going for a walk, or reading a good book. Men often feel like self-care is a luxury they can't afford, but it's vital for mental health. Whether it's getting a massage, enjoying a hobby, or simply relaxing, self-care should be a part of every man's routine.

Creating Your Own Routine: It's Not About Perfection

Remember, your routine doesn't need to be perfect or Instagram-worthy. It just needs to work for you. Start small, experiment with different practices, and adjust as needed. The key is consistency—sticking to your routine even when life gets busy will help keep your mental well-being on track.

And who knows? You might even start looking forward to your morning routine. Just don't be surprised if you end up making a cup of coffee that actually tastes good for once. That's your first win of the day.

4. Mental Health Toolkit for Men

Exercises, Tools, and Practices Specific to Men's Mental Health (Because Sometimes, the Man Cave Needs More Than Just a Couch)

Men's mental health deserves a toolkit as unique as they are—something practical, easy to use, and, most importantly, not *another* thing to add to the never-ending to-do list. So, let's take a step back and rethink how men can take control of their mental well-being without feeling like they're signing up for a month-long retreat in the Himalayas.

In this chapter, we're diving into exercises, tools, and practices that cater to men's needs specifically. Think of it as your go-to guide for when you need to de-stress, process your emotions, or just take a mental time-out. Bonus: we'll also borrow a little inspiration from the ladies and show how some of their approaches to mental wellness can be beneficial for men.

1. The Power of Journaling: Writing Your Way to Clarity

Okay, I know what you're thinking. *Journaling? That's for teenage girls and their secret diaries.* But hear me out: journaling isn't just about writing down how your day went. It's about creating a space where you can check in with yourself, unload your mental baggage, and reflect on what's going on in your life.

Journaling Prompts to Get You Started:

What's been weighing on my mind lately?
When was the last time I felt truly at peace? What was I doing?

What's one thing I can do today that will help me feel better about myself?

If I could let go of one thing that's stressing me out, what would it be?

Who are the people in my life who truly support me? How can I show them appreciation?

The great thing about journaling is that you can make it as brief or as detailed as you want. Start with five minutes a day—just jot down a few thoughts. This is a safe space for your emotions. And remember, it doesn't need to be perfect. If you're feeling a little creative, you can even draw, doodle, or write a short story about how you'd like your day to go. Who says journaling has to be serious?

2. Stress Management Techniques: How to Chill Without a Cold Beer

Stress is a silent killer—it sneaks up on you and impacts everything, from your physical health to your emotional well-being. But you don't need to let stress control your life. Here are some stress management techniques that are tailored for men and can be done without needing a "guru" or a yoga mat.

Quick Stress Relief Tools:

The "5-5-5" Breathing Exercise: Feel the stress coming on? Stop what you're doing and take five deep breaths. Breathe in for five seconds, hold for five seconds, and breathe out for five seconds. Repeat five times. Sounds simple, right? But this small shift in focus can immediately reduce stress and help you regain control.

The Power of Visualization: Close your eyes for a minute and imagine your ideal stress-free moment. Whether it's lying on a beach, watching a football game with friends, or hanging out in the man cave—let your mind wander to a place where you feel calm. It's like a mini-vacation for your brain.

Progressive Muscle Relaxation (PMR): Tension shows up in our bodies before it shows up in our minds. When you feel stressed, try PMR. Start by tensing your toes, holding for five seconds, then releasing. Work your way up to your calves, thighs, and all the way to your head. By focusing on your body's tension, you'll notice your mind calming down too.

And here's the kicker: **exercise** is a stress-busting powerhouse. Whether it's a brisk walk, lifting weights, or punching the bag at the gym, moving your body helps release endorphins, your brain's natural stress-fighting chemicals.

3. Physical Activity: Stress Relief with Some Swagger

Exercise is not just about getting swole (though that's a nice bonus). It's about improving your mood, clearing your mind, and feeling good in your body. But here's the thing—there's no need to sign up for a marathon or try to bench-press an entire truck. Physical activity can be as simple as taking a brisk walk, going for a swim, or practicing martial arts.

Movement That Works for Men:

Strength Training: The physical benefits of lifting weights are pretty well known, but did you know that lifting weights can also give your mental health a boost? Strength training helps reduce anxiety, depression, and stress by improving the body's hormone levels. Plus, there's something *very* satisfying about hitting a new personal best.

HIIT (High-Intensity Interval Training): If you're the kind of guy who likes a challenge, HIIT workouts are a quick way to burn stress while boosting your mood. It's intense, it's fast, and it leaves you feeling like a superhero. Plus, it's perfect for a guy who has about 20 minutes of free time between work and family responsibilities.

Walking or Hiking: Not into hardcore workouts? No problem. Walking (or hiking, if you're feeling adventurous) is a fantastic way to clear your mind and get your body moving without all the sweat. Bonus points if you walk outside in nature—you'll feel like a new man.

4. The Social Side: Building a Network of Support

One of the biggest advantages women have when it comes to mental health is their ability to create and maintain strong social support networks. Let's face it, women are *way* better at picking up the phone to call a friend when they're stressed out or going through a tough time. But men can—and should—do the same.

Social Strategies for Men:

Find Your Tribe: Whether it's a group of friends you can go to the pub with, a work buddy who understands your struggles, or a brother-in-law who knows how to talk about anything but politics—find people you can rely on.

Make Time for Quality Connections: Men often bond over activities, whether that's watching sports, going fishing, or working on a car. While these activities are great for connection, it's also important to check in on a deeper level. You don't have to start sharing your deepest fears, but expressing how you're feeling can create stronger, more supportive relationships.

Be Open to New Connections: If you don't have a close-knit support system, it's time to create one. Whether that's joining a new club, volunteering for a cause, or reconnecting with old friends, the key is to put yourself out there and nurture those relationships.

5. Borrowing from Women's Mental Wellness Toolkit

It's not just about following a checklist—men can take inspiration from women's approaches to mental health, particularly when it comes to emotional awareness and seeking support. Women tend to be more open to discussing their emotions, seeking help when needed, and building a strong social network. Men can learn from these practices, making their mental health journey a little smoother.

Women also prioritize self-care in a way that men sometimes overlook. Making time for relaxation, setting boundaries, and learning to say "no" when needed is something both men and women should practice.

Wrapping It Up: Your Mental Health is a Tool—Use It

Incorporating these strategies into your life doesn't mean you'll be an emotional genius overnight (trust me, I'm not there yet either). But the important thing is taking small steps every day to nurture your mental well-being. With the right mindset and the right tools, you'll be able to tackle whatever comes your way without burning out.

So, go ahead—use this toolkit to your advantage. Start journaling, take a breather when you need it, get your body moving, and surround yourself with people who support you. Your mental health will thank you for it.

Conclusion: Embracing Midlife as a Journey of Growth and Fulfillment

As we close the book on this exploration of men's mental health after 40, it's important to remember that midlife is not a crisis—it's a **moment of transformation**. It's an opportunity to redefine who you are, to make peace with the past, and to look forward to the future with a sense of possibility.

We've unpacked the unique challenges men face in their 40s—from the weight of societal expectations to the pressures of career and family, the struggle with stress, and the sometimes-overlooked issue of loneliness. But we've also explored practical tools and strategies to help you manage these challenges. Whether it's through journaling, exercise, or building deeper connections, the keys to maintaining your mental well-being are right at your fingertips.

Here's the key takeaway:

Prioritize your mental health. It's not a luxury. It's essential. Taking care of your mind is just as important as taking care of your body. It's about **embracing vulnerability**, understanding your emotions, and creating a life that works for you—not according to some outdated blueprint.

Remember, midlife doesn't have to be the end of your journey. In fact, it's the **beginning of a new chapter**—one where you get to rediscover what truly matters to you, challenge yourself in new ways, and build the life you want. You've earned the wisdom that comes with experience. You've lived through the ups and downs, and now, you're in a prime position to put that knowledge to work for your own growth and fulfillment.

So, **take a deep breath,** let go of any outdated expectations, and step boldly into this exciting new phase. You've got everything it takes to thrive in midlife and beyond. It's your time—embrace it, own it, and make it count.

CHAPTER NINE

A Guided 30-Day Plan for Mental Well-Being

Week 1: Awareness & Small Wins

- **Day 1:** *Acceptance Mode On* – You're here. You're 40+. Now what? No panic, just deep breaths.

- **Day 2:** *Ditch the Superman Cape* – You don't have to do everything alone. Make a list of things you can delegate (yes, even at home).

- **Day 3:** *10-Minute Meditation* – If you can sit in a car stuck in traffic, you can sit quietly and breathe for 10 minutes.

- **Day 4:** *Journaling for the Brave* – Write down your thoughts, even if it's just "Why am I doing this?"

- **Day 5:** *Reconnect with an Old Friend* – Not just a WhatsApp forward, but an actual conversation.

- **Day 6:** *Tech Detox for 2 Hours* – No phone, no news, no doom-scrolling. Your brain will thank you.

- **Day 7:** *Laugh at Yourself* – Watch a comedy, recall an embarrassing moment, or just look at your teenage hairstyle pictures.

Week 2: Emotional Strength & Stress Management

- **Day 8:** *Gratitude List* – Write three things you're grateful for. "At least I still have hair" counts.

- **Day 9:** *Mindful Eating* – Chew. Slowly. Yes, really.

- **Day 10:** *Move That Body* – No need for an extreme workout. Walk, stretch, or just dance badly when no one's watching.

- **Day 11:** *Address One Unfinished Task* – That one thing you've been avoiding? Do it. No more mental clutter.

- **Day 12:** *Breathing Techniques* – Try deep belly breathing when stress hits instead of reaching for caffeine.

- **Day 13:** *Express Yourself* – Say what you feel. To your spouse, kids, even your dog. (The dog will love it.)

- **Day 14:** *Solo Date* – Treat yourself to a coffee, a movie, or just a peaceful drive.

Week 3: Relationships & Social Health

- **Day 15:** *Apologize Where Necessary* – If you owe someone an apology, give it. Your ego will survive.

- **Day 16:** *Surprise Gesture* – Do something unexpected for your partner, parents, or kids.

- **Day 17:** *Connect with a Supportive Group* – Join a men's circle, a hobby group, or just talk to like-minded people.

- **Day 18:** *Boundaries, My Friend!* – Say no where needed, and stop overcommitting.

- **Day 19:** *Try Something New* – A new recipe, a hobby, a sport. Surprise yourself.

- **Day 20:** *Silent Observation* – Listen more, speak less. See what happens.

- **Day 21:** *Social Media Detox* – One day without social media. Hard? Maybe. Worth it? Definitely.

Week 4: Spiritual & Mental Strength

- **Day 22:** *Meditation Upgrade* – Try a guided session or chant a mantra for 5 minutes.

- **Day 23:** *Declutter Your Space* – A clean space helps a clean mind.

- **Day 24:** *Laugh with Family* – Share old stories, pull out childhood pictures, relive happy times.

- **Day 25:** *Reassess Your Goals* – Are you on the right path? Small changes can lead to big results.

- **Day 26:** *Let Go of a Past Resentment* – It's heavy. Drop it.

- **Day 27:** *Step into Nature* – A simple walk outside can reset your mood.

- **Day 28:** *Write a Letter to Yourself* – Reflect on how you feel now compared to Day 1.

- **Day 29:** *Affirmation Day* – Say something positive to yourself and believe it.

- **Day 30:** *Celebrate Your Progress* – You made it! What's your biggest takeaway?

CHAPTER TEN

The Death of the First Man

Letting Go of Who You Thought You Were

There comes a moment in every man's life when he realizes that the identity he has spent decades building no longer fits.

Maybe it happens when your career plateaus, and you realize you've been running on autopilot, chasing goals that no longer excite you. Maybe it's in your marriage, where conversations have been replaced with logistics and intimacy with routine. Maybe it's in your own body—where injuries linger longer, where strength is harder to maintain, where the face in the mirror carries a fatigue you can't quite explain.

Or maybe it's something more subtle. A vague, persistent sense that the man you were—the ambitious, driven, fire-filled version of yourself—is slipping away.

This is the death of the first man.

CHAPTER ELEVEN

The Unraveling of the Mask

You spent years constructing this identity. It served you well. It pushed you to achieve, to survive, to build. But now, it's starting to crack.

A man in his late 40s once told me: "I climbed the ladder my entire life, only to realize it was leaning against the wrong wall."

You know this feeling. The creeping thought that the things you worked so hard for might not be the things that truly matter.

And yet, letting go of this identity is terrifying. Because if you are not this—the achiever, the provider, the man who has it all together—then who are you?

This is why so many men resist change. They double down on old patterns, chasing external validation to silence the growing doubt. They tell themselves that if they just earn a little more, buy a little more, work a little harder, things will fall back into place.

But they won't. Because this is not a problem to be solved. It is a transformation waiting to happen.

The Fall Before the Rebirth

The death of the first man is painful. It is filled with discomfort, uncertainty, and moments of raw vulnerability.

For some, it leads to anger—lashing out at the world, blaming others for the discontent that lingers beneath the surface. For others, it leads to withdrawal—numbing through distractions, avoiding difficult conversations, retreating into themselves.

But for those who are willing to face it, to let the old self die, something remarkable happens.

In the emptiness that follows, a new man begins to emerge.

This man is no longer driven by the need to prove himself. He is no longer afraid of uncertainty. He begins to understand that his worth is not tied to his achievements, but to the depth of his presence in his own life.

This is the first step in your journey. The shedding of old skin. The willingness to stand in the unknown and trust that something greater awaits on the other side.

The question now is: Are you ready to let go?

Becoming the Second Man – A New Vision for Life Beyond 40

The Second Man is the evolved version of yourself—someone who no longer lives just for external validation but starts seeking internal fulfillment. This is the phase where priorities shift from competition to contentment, from proving to improving, from chasing to embracing.

The journey beyond 40 isn't about decline; it's about **evolution**. The **Second Man** is wiser, calmer, and finally, truly himself. Instead of running in the race society sets, he starts running toward what actually fulfills him.

CHAPTER THIRTEEN

Final Thoughts: A New Beginning Beyond 40

Congratulations! You've made it through this book, and more importantly, you've taken the first step toward understanding and prioritizing your mental well-being. Midlife isn't a crisis—it's an evolution. It's a chance to redefine masculinity, embrace change, and finally do the things that truly matter to you.

Remember, you don't have to carry every burden alone. Seeking help, finding balance, and focusing on your emotional and physical health is not a sign of weakness—it's a sign of wisdom. Whether it's building stronger relationships, managing stress, or simply laughing more, small steps can lead to a big transformation.

If there's one takeaway from this book, let it be this: Midlife is not the beginning of the end—it's the start of something new, something better. You've got this! Now go out there and live *beyond* 40 with confidence, joy, and peace of mind.

About The Author

I am the author of six Amazon No.1 Bestsellers, spanning diverse genres from mythology and poetry (in both Hindi and English) to relationships and personal growth. Writing has been my passion since early childhood, a journey that has led me to explore and share wisdom through my books.

With an insatiable curiosity and a love for learning, I continuously update myself with the evolving world—both in thought and in practice. My latest work, Beyond 40: The Unfinished Story, is an extension of this passion, delving into a subject often overlooked: men's emotional and mental struggles in midlife.

In today's world, men face silent battles that few acknowledge. While society and legal frameworks have evolved to protect women, men often find themselves without the same emotional or legal support. Many struggle in silence, some surrendering to their circumstances, and, tragically, some finding no way forward. This realization compelled me to write this book—to give voice to their struggles, break the stigma, and offer guidance on navigating midlife with strength and resilience.

Through my writings, I not only share knowledge but also real-life experiences—both my own and those of others—hoping to inspire, heal, and empower my readers.